Happy 16th Birthday

OVER...
YOUR HIDDEN FEARS

Please N.B.

> When hope is gone,
> And you're in despair,
> Almost like God,
> Friends are everywhere.

P.T.L
Paul

[Roman Ch8:28]

OVERCOMING
YOUR HIDDEN FEARS

H. Norman Wright

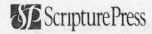
Scripture Press

Amersham-on-the-Hill, Bucks HP6 6JQ, England.

© 1989 by H. Norman Wright
First published in the USA 1985 as Uncovering Your Hidden Fears by
Tyndale House Publishers, Inc., Wheaton, Illinois, USA

First British edition 1990

ISBN 1 872059 36 8

Scripture quotations, unless otherwise noted, are
from *The Holy Bible*, New International Version.
Copyright © 1973, 1978, 1984 International Bible Society.
Published by Hodder & Stoughton.

Scripture quotations marked AMP are from
The Amplified Bible. Old Testament copyright © 1965, 1987
by The Zondervan Corporation. *The Amplified New Testament*
copyright © 1958, 1987 by The Lockman Foundation.
Used by permission.

Scripture quotations marked RSV are taken from
The Holy Bible, Revised Standard Version. Copyright
1946, 1952, 1971 by the Division of Christian Education of the
National Council of the Churches of Christ in the USA.
Used by permission.

Designed and Printed in England for
SCRIPTURE PRESS FOUNDATION (UK) LTD
Raans Road, Amersham-on-the-Hill, Bucks HP6 6JQ by
Nuprint Ltd, 30b Station Road, Harpenden, Herts AL5 4SE.

Contents

ONE
Are You Imprisoned by Fear?

The fear of life is worse than the fear of death.
Fear cripples our relationships with others.
Fear makes life a chore.

"Do not fear, for I am with you; do not be dismayed, for I am your God." (Isa. 41:10)

The jagged stone and concrete walls were immense, towering forty feet high and measuring seven feet thick. Atop the barrier rose an additional four feet of menacing barbed wire. Within the fortress-like enclosure loomed several large, uninviting concrete buildings, each sparsely adorned and almost windowless.

Inside one of the buildings, three men stood before an electronically controlled metal door. Two of them were dressed in uniform, but the man between them was garbed in ill-fitting, faded denim. The door slid open with a grinding hum, revealing a dark hallway flanked by small cells, which stretched several hundred feet to the end of the building. The men entered the corridor. The sounds of their footsteps—two men marching confidently and one man shuffling hesitantly—echoed throughout the building. Silent faces peered through the barred cell doors as the men passed.

Finally, they reached an open cell crowded with two bunks, a sink, and a toilet. The prisoner sighed heavily, then entered and turned to face the guards. The electronic door slowly closed, locking with a loud *clank*.

The gloomy cell would be this prisoner's living quarters for the rest of his life. He had been tried, found guilty, sentenced, and now imprisoned. Why? Because he had deliberately and willfully terminated the life of another person. He would live out his natural life denied the opportunities, pleasures, and experiences of normal life. Tragic. Didn't he realize what he was doing when he committed the crime? Why didn't he choose to act differently? What a terrible existence he has brought upon himself! What could be worse than being confined to prison?

Yes, this man received the punishment he deserved, unfortunately for him. But even more unfortunate are the millions of individuals today who have sentenced themselves to mental and emotional prisons of their own making. They have not committed crimes, they have not stood trial, and they have not been sentenced to prison by a court of law. Yet millions today have effectively locked themselves away from life's opportunities, pleasures, and experiences. Perhaps you also find yourself incarcerated in this prison.

It's the prison of fear.

Each day I talk with people whose lives are filled with fear. Some of them have just developed their fears; others have lived in a prison of fear since childhood. The good news is that, unlike the experience of the prisoner in our story, the prison doors to fear are unlocked! No matter how long you have been imprisoned behind its bars, you *can* conquer fear and walk away from it.

Normal and abnormal fear

All of us are afraid sometimes. That's normal. But some of us are fearful most of the time. That's *not* normal.

We were not created to live in fear or to dread life, yet some of us do. We were not designed to be motivated or driven by fear, yet some of us are.

Occasionally, people tell me that they are afraid of death. That's quite common. But even more people I talk to are afraid of life. Living life to its full potential is a threat to them. They are emotionally paralyzed and refuse to participate in many of life's normal experiences. When counseling them, I often suggest, "It seems you are immobilized by fear," and they agree!

There is a difference between being afraid and being immobilized by fear. We may be afraid at times, but we are not to abound in fear. Paul wrote: "For God did not give us a spirit of timidity [fear], but a spirit of power, of love and of self-discipline" (2 Tim. 1:7). How strange it is for Christians to choose to imprison themselves in fear, especially when Christ came to set captives free! We have freedom in Christ, yet we often choose to walk through life in a mobile cell of fear, shut away from people and experiences.

The fear of life is actually more debilitating than the fear of death. Fear disables. Fear shortens life. Fear cripples our relationships with others. Fear blocks our relationship with God. Fear makes life a chore. We become the living dead! John Haggai describes it well:

> Having a fear is like having a cancer. It is always there, hidden inside you, always sapping your strength and breaking your concentration. Even rational fear can be destructive in its effects. What is popularly called "shell shock," for instance, is really nothing of the kind. It is a form of mental breakdown resulting from the prolonged endurance of rational fear—a conflict, if you will, between a soldier's natural fear on the battlefield and the sense of duty (or perhaps the fear of punishment for not performing it) that makes him stay there.
>
> You cannot hide fear. Its destruction begins by feeding on you, and then moving into your social and physical environment.[1]

The fear of life is the fear of being hurt, being rejected, making a mistake, showing our imperfections, and failing as a person. Somewhere along our path in life we subconsciously decide not to be vulnerable and never to take a risk. Before long we become turtles tucked inside a defensive shell of fear, immobile and detached from life. Like the turtle, we will only progress in life when we stick our necks out. Similarly, the lobster cannot mate or increase in size until it sheds its protective shell. When it does, the lobster is vulnerable to attack from its enemies. But without that risk the species would die off. We must shed our shells of fear if we are to survive and grow.

The roots of fear

Our English word *fear* comes from the Old English *faer*, meaning "sudden calamity or danger." Fear has come to mean the emotional response to real or imagined danger. The Hebrew word for fear can also be translated *dread*, a heavy oppressive sensation of fear. A word we often interchange with *fear* is *anxiety*, which comes from the Latin *anxius*. To be anxious is to be troubled in mind about some uncertain event. A variation of *anxius* means "to press tightly or to strangle." Anxiety is often a suffocating experience.

Fear and anxiety are actually quite similar. A true fear has an identifiable object of danger, either real (a burglar in your house) or imagined (a shadow that looks like a burglar). When we're anxious, we have the same feeling of fear, but we don't know why. The danger is subconscious.

Our language is rich in terms that describe fear, anxiety, and related emotional responses. *Timidity* describes a perpetual tendency toward fear, and *panic* is a sudden upsurge of terror. Consider several other terms in the vocabulary of fear. Which of these best describes your feelings when fear strikes?

apprehension	uneasiness	nervousness
worry	disquiet	solicitude
concern	misgiving	qualm
edginess	jitteriness	sensitivity
wary	unnerved	unsettled
upset	aghast	distress
agitation	perturbation	consternation
trepidation	scare	fright
dread	terror	horror
alarm	panic	anguish

Blowing fear out of proportion

Recently a friend and I were fishing at a mountain lake. We were working on a nice string of fish when it started to rain, and in just a few minutes the shower became a downpour. We hated to leave our excellent fishing spot, but we decided that dry was better than wet. So we climbed into my friend's car and drove up the highway.

As we ascended to a higher elevation the rain turned to snow, and soon the snowstorm was heavy and intense. As we crested a slight hill the car started into an uncontrollable spin on the slippery road. I realized we were sliding helplessly toward a roadside cliff, so I reached to unbuckle my seat belt in order to jump out before the car slid over the edge. But in a few seconds the car came to a stop in the middle of the road.

The life-threatening danger had ceased, but my friend and I had been plunged into a state of fear. There was nothing we could do about the way our bodies reacted; we had accelerated heart rates, a sinking feeling in our stomachs, and white, blood-drained skin. We stayed on edge emotionally as we crept slowly and cautiously down the hill into town, briefly losing control of the car on two other curves.

Our experience on the icy road illustrates a legitimate and rational fear: We could have lost our lives. But many who are imprisoned by irrational fear would exaggerate the dangers of our close call and swear never again to go fishing, drive on a mountain road, or drive in snow. Someone has said that an exaggerated fear is equipped with binoculars. It tends to magnify dangers that are a great distance away, making small threats appear large.

Normal fear reacts, but exaggerated fear *over*reacts. In southern California, we seem to have more than our share of danger and violence: freeway shooting, gang wars, the infamous Hillside Strangler, and so forth. Most Californians react normally to these dangers by being cautious on the freeways and avoiding some potentially dangerous areas of the city. But those suffering from exaggerated fear overreact by confining themselves to their homes or neighborhoods or by selling their property and leaving the state altogether.

I can think of another example of exaggerated fear that may be more common. Picture yourself as a student who faces a final exam that will have a major impact on your course grade. You dread each step toward the classroom, and a cloud of fear hangs over you as you wait for the exam booklets to be distributed. You complete your exam, but you finish well ahead of anyone else. You begin to wonder, "Perhaps I didn't write enough. Maybe I didn't know as much as I needed to know. Why is everyone else taking so much longer to finish?"

The more you think about it, the greater your fear of failing the exam grows. You wait until others turn in their exams, then you stand and take your booklet to the front desk. Outside the classroom, you notice small groups of students discussing the exam and comparing answers. You are tempted to join in, but you're afraid you might discover you blew the exam, so you leave. The fear of knowing the results keeps you bound by apprehension for the next two days until the class meets again and the results are made known.

When you enter the classroom, you hear the low buzz of irritation among the students. The exams have not been graded! You are forced to wait until the next class meeting for the final verdict. Part of you is disappointed; you want to get it over with. But part of you is relieved because you don't have to face the results yet. A low-level fear continues to permeate your consciousness. You feel like the person described in Proverbs 12:25: "An anxious heart weighs a man down."

Finally, during the following class session, the graded exams are returned. As your booklet is passed to you, the same sense of dread you experienced when you took the exam returns. You keep the booklet closed for a moment, then hold your breath as you open it to find the grade—a solid *B!* A faint smile brightens your face, and your entire body relaxes as you begin to experience life again. You chide yourself, "Why was I so uptight over this exam? I breezed through it."

Yes, why do exaggerated fears abound over such common

activities as exams, job applications, and performance reviews? It's because we're afraid of failure, ridicule, and not making the grade in our own eyes or the eyes of others. All of us want to feel adequate in all areas of life. We're afraid we might not be as proficient as we had hoped.

We must realize that *every normal fear has the potential to become an exaggerated fear*. What exaggerated fears have hounded you in the past? What fears are exaggerated in your life right now? What normal fears threaten to become exaggerated fears in the future?

Pushed around by fear

Fear is strange. It can prompt us to a certain action and, at the same time, prevent us from completing that action. Over the years, I've talked to numerous men in their forties and fifties who admit to fearful concerns about their health. Often the fear over personal health is a two-headed monster—pulling us in two directions at the same time. John's story has been repeated many times over:

> Most of my life, I've been in good health. But several months ago, I began feeling tired most of the time. I didn't even have the energy for the activities I enjoyed. I discovered a few minor aches and pains—nothing specific, but many of them were in my chest.
>
> I knew I should go see my doctor. Part of me wanted to go, but I used excuse after excuse to put it off: I didn't have time, the pain would go away eventually, the pain was all in my head, etc.
>
> Then I figured it out: I was actually afraid to see my doctor. I was afraid he would find a major problem. Part of me wanted to know if there was a problem, but part of me didn't. I finally made an appointment.
>
> When the technicians and nurses were taking the tests, I watched their facial expressions to see if I could learn anything about the results. No response. I asked, "How

did it turn out?" and they said they would tabulate the results and let me know.

I remember the day I went to hear the results. A battle raged inside me. I was afraid to hear the news, but I was also afraid *not* to hear the news. And it turned out to be good news! Fear had prodded me to take action, then acted like an anchor holding me back. I never realized how much fear can jerk someone around.[2]

Four kinds of fear

Do you realize there are only four basic kinds of fear? Grouping our various fears into categories will help us take the necessary action to keep fear from plaguing our lives.

1. Fears of Things and Places. The most easily identifiable fears are the fears of things and places, commonly called phobias. The list of phobias is almost endless, but here are several of the most common:

acrophobia	fear of heights
aquaphobia	fear of water
astraphobia	fear of lightning
brontophobia	fear of thunder
cancerphobia	fear of cancer
claustrophobia	fear of closed spaces
melissophobia	fear of bees
mysophobia	fear of dirt, germs, contamination
nycotophobia	fear of darkness or night
ophidiophobia	fear of snakes
pathophobia	fear of illness
zoophobia	fear of animals

Read through the list again. As you do, place a *C* beside any phobias that haunted you as a child, a *T* beside any you experienced as a teen, and an *A* beside any you struggle with as an adult. Also, write down any phobias you have experienced that are not mentioned, whether you know the technical names for them or not.

Many of our phobias can be dealt with by simply avoiding the objects or situations we fear. If you are ophidiophobic, you don't go where snakes live or are kept. If you are claustrophobic, you take the stairs instead of confining yourself to an elevator.

But some events are out of our control, and phobias in these areas are more difficult to overcome. For example, living in southern California, I have endured many earthquakes over the years. And I have counseled numerous individuals whose fear of earthquakes has dominated their lives. Their phobic reactions include avoiding newspapers or news programs for fear they might learn about even the slightest earthquake that occurred nearby. Some refuse to move back into their homes for weeks following a minor earthquake.

The drought of 1988 in our country will be long remembered, especially in several states that remained parched and dusty for weeks on end. Newspapers reported that the drought toll could be measured in fear as well as dollars. As the crops withered, businesses associated with farming also began to dry up. Anxiety and fear spread like dust on the wind. A hardware dealer in South Dakota reported he had never been as scared as he was during the drought. He and thousands like him were at the mercy of the weather. During the depths of the problem he said, "Each night I wake up and lie there for hours in fear of what is going to happen, and I desperately try to figure out what we are going to do."

Many events in life are out of our control. And some, like earthquakes and droughts, persist in feeding our anxiety daily.

2. Fear of People. The most difficult fears to recognize are those associated with people and social interaction. These include the fear of rejection, anger, disapproval, failure, and success. Almost everybody experiences these fears at one time or another. They drive us and control us more than we realize. You may be driven by one or more of these fears right now and not even be aware of it.

There are two reasons why interpersonal fears are difficult to identify. First, many people recognize the presence of fear, but devote all their efforts to justifying it as a reasonable or legitimate emotion. For example, an employee's fear of his boss's disapproval keeps him awake nights and feeds his ulcer. But instead of admitting his fear, the employee talks about his inner drive to be loyal to his boss.

Second, the fear of people is difficult to spot because those who suffer from it strategically avoid all situations and events where it might surface. For example, the individual who is afraid of crowds always has a "schedule conflict" when invited to a party, and he or she may attend weddings but never stays for the reception. Interpersonal fears never come to light if you constantly avoid contact with people.

3. Fear of Fear. Did you know that some people are afraid of their fears? They actually fear the sensation of fear itself, and so they go out of their way to avoid all places and situations that produce these sensations. Since they cannot avoid the involuntary knot in the stomach or the flushed complexion that accompanies a frightening experience, they avoid any setting in which it might possibly occur.

4. Fear of Thoughts. There is another group of individuals who may not be afraid of their feelings but are afraid of their thoughts. Have you ever frantically wished that a frightening thought would go away—or would never have entered your mind in the first place? Occasional thoughts like these are normal and relatively harmless, but the persistent fear of these thoughts is abnormal.

Useless fears vs. useful fears

Some of our fears are useful to us, but most of them are useless. If our useless fears had only a brief life span, we could tolerate them. The problem is that useless fears tend to hang on for years; some even follow us to the grave. It's not the fear that bothers us; it's the consequences of the fear.

A useful fear is one that prompts us to action in the face of a real threat. If I'm driving down the highway and a car traveling in the opposite direction swerves into my lane, the fear that strikes me is useful, prompting me to take evasive action. If I feel pains in my chest, jaw, and left arm, the sudden fear of a heart attack is useful, driving me to seek immediate medical attention. If I'm strolling along a trail in the Grand Teton National-al Park (as I often do) and come face to face with a 600-pound bear, my momentary terror is useful, spurring me to put as much distance as possible between the bear and me. If I read in the newspaper that the savings bank in which I have deposited my money is about to fold, my fear is useful, encouraging me to rescue my savings immediately.

A useful fear, like a depression, is an inner warning system alerting me that something is going wrong in my life. A useful fear signals a real danger that must be confronted with corrective action. A lawyer once shared with me that he experienced a persistent, low-level fear of failing his bar exam. But this useful fear pushed him to study diligently for the exam, which he passed.

The Bible tells us that a reverential fear of God is a useful fear because it leads to wisdom. Jesus Christ graphically described the useful fear of God in Matthew 10:28: "Do not be afraid of those who kill the body but cannot kill the soul. Rather, be afraid of the One who can destroy both soul and body in hell."

Paul Tournier, the Swiss psychiatrist, had an interesting perspective of fear in the life of the Christian:

> Thus fear is beneficial or harmful, according to whether or not it plays in our lives the part assigned to it in the purpose of God. The biblical perspective never suggests that we should pass over from the camp of the weak to that of the strong, but that we should recognize our weakness. If we find it so difficult to confess our fears, that is because we always want to seem strong. We are ashamed of our fear, and this shame consolidates the fear and renders it harmful. A woman patient of mine, suffering from a tumor in the breast, writes to me about her fear of cancer: "A real

Christian ought not to be afraid." No, madam, the Christian is not exempt from fear, but he takes his fears to God. Faith does not suppress fear; what it does is to allow one to go forward in spite of it.[3]

A conversation I recently overheard between a man and woman illustrates the healthy respect we need to have for useful fears. They were discussing a life-threatening experience that faced them. The man asked, "Aren't you afraid?" The woman's response was tinged with anger:

> Of course, I'm afraid! What kind of person do you think I am? It isn't sensible not to be afraid when there is good reason for it. I was afraid when I was beaten as a child. I was afraid when my husband left me. I've spent a lot of my life being afraid. Show me someone who hasn't! That's why so many people resort to drugs and alcohol. It blots out their fear. There is nothing so outstanding about having fear as long as you don't *act* fearful—as long as you don't allow yourself to become crippled into doing nothing because of your fear. We've got to face our fear and move ahead.[4]

Some fears simply get in the way and become useless to us. Some fears can cause us to do the very thing we fear. They can take the pleasure out of life and limit our productivity. Some fears that are initially useful can become too intense and thus become useless to us.

How do useless fears develop? Is there any pattern to them? Does everyone suffer from useless fears? Here are a few facts to keep in mind:

1. Everyone can develop useless fears; no one is immune to them.
2. Highly emotional people tend to experience a greater sense of anxiety and fear.

3. A person who experiences an early fearful situation at a vulnerable stage will be more likely to develop fears later in life if similar experiences occur.

"Fear not"

Often my fishing buddy and I hike into one of the backcountry lakes to catch trout. One of the lakes we fish is nestled in a small valley surrounded by massive mountains. On occasion, my friend will fish a distance away from me and I must yell to get his attention. My shouted hello in that natural echo chamber comes back to me as "hello . . . hello . . . hello" in decreasing volume.

Similarly, a loud and clear command to Christians on the subject of useless fears echoes throughout the Scriptures. We find the words *fear not* 366 times in the Bible. Frequently they are followed by a reminder of God's presence in our lives that precludes any reasons for useless fears. The words of Jesus echo throughout the New Testament and into our daily lives. During your most intense bouts with fear, allow your mind to operate like an echo chamber. Instead of letting your fears reverberate within that chamber, let the words of Scripture continually echo—"fear not . . . fear not . . . fear not."

TWO

Are You Keeping Your Fears Alive?

Fear compels us forward while inhibiting our progress at the same time.

Fear is like a videotape continually replaying our most haunting experiences.

Hope allows God's Spirit to set us free from our fears and to draw us forward in our lives.

". . . We who have fled to take hold of the hope offered to us may be greatly encouraged. We have this hope as an anchor for the soul, firm and secure." (Heb. 6:18-19)

Joan was a middle-aged, well-groomed, successful woman who came to me for counseling. She did not display the normal apprehension that so many people experience during an initial counseling session. She communicated very well, and she was alert and polished in her manner. You would never guess from Joan's appearance and accomplishments the extent of the fear festering inside her that she admitted to me that day. When I remarked about her outward control and composure, Joan replied, "*No one* is aware of the fear I live with. I am very capable of hiding it."

As we continued to talk, I asked her, "How is it that a person as capable and successful as you is so wracked by fear? And how have you accomplished so much while carrying such a load of fear?"

Joan's answer amazed me: "That's just it—I'm motivated by fear! Fear drives me; it keeps me going. I don't like being controlled by fear, but I wonder if I would accomplish anything if I were not motivated by it."

Driven by fear. I wonder how many people are driven, like Joan, by the fears of their lives. It seems like such a negative way to be motivated. In some ways a fear-driven life-style can be very effective. But there is a high cost for such a negative drive.

22

Two motivating forces

There are two great motivating forces in life: fear and hope. Interestingly, both of these motivators can produce the same results. Fear is a powerful *negative* drive. It compels us forward while inhibiting our progress at the same time. Fear is like a noose that slowly tightens around your neck if you move in the wrong direction. Fear restricts your abilities and thoughts and leads you toward panic reactions. Even when you are standing on the threshold of success, your most creative and inventive plans can be sabotaged by fear.

Fear is also like a videotape continually replaying our most haunting experiences: embarrassing moments, rejections, failures, hurts, and disappointments. The message of the fear video is clear: Life is full of these experiences, and they *will* repeat themselves. Fear causes us to say, "I can't do it; I may fail."

Hope is a totally different motivating force—a *positive* drive. Hope is like a magnet that draws you toward your goal. Hope expands your life and brings a message of possibility and change. It draws you away from the bad experiences of the past and toward better experiences in the future. The hope video continually replays scenarios of potential success. Hope causes us to say, "I can do it; I will succeed."

What motivates you? What drives you? What pushes you ahead in life: fear or hope?

The motivational power of fear is clearly seen in some primitive cultures of the world where voodoo is practiced. In his book *The Mind-Body Effect*, Dr. Herbert Benson of the Harvard Medical School describes voodoo practices to illustrate the relationship between the human mind and body. Voodoo was originally a form of ancestor worship that is believed to have started in Africa. In the Australian aboriginal tribes, witch doctors often cast voodoo spells on people that led to disease and death. You can imagine the fear that controlled people in these cultures.

Dr. Benson gives a documented example of a young aborigine who slept at a friend's home while on a trip. The young man had been forbidden by his elders to eat wild hen under voodoo threat of death. So at breakfast the young man asked his older host if the meal he was about to eat was wild hen. The dish *was* wild hen, but his friend replied, "Of course not." So the young man ate his breakfast and went on his way unaware and unaffected.

Years passed, and once again the two friends met. During their conversation, the older man told his friend about the joke he played on him by serving him wild hen during his visit. The younger man's fears immediately came to the surface. He began to shake with terror, and within twenty-four hours he was dead.[1]

Numerous cases such as this one have been documented over the years. Although it may be an extreme example of the destructive power of fear, it illustrates the negative effect our fears can have on our lives.

Feeding your fears

In working with fearful clients, I sometimes ask, "What do you do to keep your fear alive?"

Usually their expressions register shock as they respond, "I can't believe you asked me that question! What do you mean 'alive'? I'm trying to kill off my fear, not help it grow! I want it dead and buried."

But I persist with my question. Why? Because most fearful individuals develop behaviors that actually feed their fears. And when a fear is fed, it doesn't diminish—it grows. One of the most important facts to keep in mind about fear is this: *The more you give in to your fears, the more they will grow*.

There are numerous ways by which fearful people keep fear alive. As we consider these characteristic behaviors, see if any of them fits your response to fear in your life.

The Avoider. Some people work very hard to avoid the object of their fear. One client had a tremendous fear of large trucks. She expended an unbelievable amount of time and energy making sure her route of travel each day was free from trucks. Side streets, out-of-the-way roads, and even alleys became part of her daily itinerary to make sure she avoided meeting any large trucks. Did her avoidance of trucks lessen her fear? No! Her daily ordeal only intensified her fear. Avoiders are motivated by fear.

The Runaway. The runaway will enter the arena of fearful experiences, but escapes as soon as possible without giving his fear a chance to diminish. A businessman was afraid of business meetings and conventions where others in his profession congregated. He was afraid his peers would discover how inept he was (or thought he was) at his job. But he was required to attend these gatherings. So, tense with fear, he would arrive at a meeting, move quickly through the room to be seen by others, and then quietly leave. Every time he did this his fear increased. And the amount of mental energy he expended on these encounters also intensified his fear. Runaways are motivated by fear.

The Doomsayer. Whenever doomsayers think about fearful situations, they focus on and exaggerate the worst possible consequences. The possibility of something bad occurring may be extremely remote, but doomsayers always expect problems. Their negativism consumes their attention.

Recently I heard some examples about partygoers that graphically illustrate the doomsayer's tendencies. Some people are very uncomfortable at parties. When a fearful doomsayer is invited to a party, his fears begin to stir and fester, and he thinks about everything he could do wrong:

- He'll go to the party on the wrong day.
- He'll go to the wrong address.
- He'll arrive too early.
- He'll arrive too late.
- He'll arrive on time, but no other guests will be there, and he will have to carry on a conversation with a boring host.
- He'll be overdressed or underdressed for the occasion.

These are just for starters! Doomsayers also fear their entrance at a party, anticipate spilling food or beverages, dread getting locked in the bathroom, and are nervous about leaving the party gracefully.

When a doomsayer hosts a party, a new range of fears comes

to light. After the initial fear that no guests will show up, other fears arise:

- The guests will be too early.
- The guests will be too late.
- The early-arriving guests will be wallflowers, and the conversation will be awkward.
- He will run out of refreshments.
- Some guests will get sick on the *hors d'oeuvres*.
- He will burn something, and the smoke alarm will sound. Guests will run for the exit; someone will be trampled, break a leg, and sue the host.
- Someone will show up that he didn't invite.
- Someone will show up drunk.

And the list goes on. Ridiculous? Yes, but to some people these fears are very real, stealing the joy from their lives. Doomsayers are motivated by fear.

The Manipulator. This clever individual enlists the help of others as cushions against fearful situations. One man was terrified of dogs. Before he went to visit someone for the first time, he called in advance to see if they had a dog. If so, he asked the hosts to keep the dog outside or at least out of sight.

Another person was afraid of fainting in elevators. Whenever she had to ride an elevator, she would turn to someone else—whether she knew him or not—and explain her problem. "I tend to pass out in elevators," she explained. "If I appear to be getting dizzy, please take hold of my arm." You can imagine the attention she received every time she stepped into an elevator! Actually, she had never passed out in an elevator, but her fear was real. Manipulators are motivated by fear.

The Non-coper. This person will actually become involved in fearful situations, but his thoughts are consumed by his fear. If he is afraid of crowds, he may be able to enter a room with fifty other people, but he might as well be there alone. He can't tell you about the other people in the room. He is so immobilized in this setting that, if he has some responsibility, he will blow it.

He will become tongue-tied, drop whatever he is serving, or forget his thought in the middle of a sentence.

I've been in a number of classrooms where a student stopped cold in the middle of his presentation and stared at his classmates in fright. The inability of these students to cope is usually traced back to the abundance of fear in their minds. That which they feared the most had come upon them—*and they made it happen themselves by plunging unprepared into a fearful situation!* Non-copers are motivated by fear.

The Silent Martyr. The fears of a silent martyr are kept totally hidden from others. Instead of being honest about his fears, this person contrives creative, legitimate-sounding excuses for not participating in a fearful situation. A parent who was deathly afraid of the water could not avoid occasionally taking her children to the beach or to the pool. But she had a vast array of excuses that kept her away from the water: It was too hot or too cold; she didn't want to risk a sunburn; she preferred to lie around and read, and so forth. Her excuses were certainly reasonable, but they were merely a smoke screen for the sense of terror she had hidden for more than twenty years. And each year her fear escalated in intensity. Silent martyrs are motivated by fear.[2]

Fear's negative focus

A person who is motivated by fear will think more about what can go wrong that what can go right. This will cause that individual to live defensively, expecting the worst, overreacting, and being immobilized. When you concentrate on what you fear or want to avoid, you increase the likelihood of its happening. Does that sound far-fetched? It really isn't.

During the deciding game of the 1950 World Series, Warren Spahn of the Milwaukee Braves was getting ready to pitch to Elston Howard, the power-hitting catcher of the New York Yankees. The Braves' manager walked out to the mound and gave Spahn some simple advice: "Don't pitch him high and outside; he'll knock the ball out of sight." Spahn tried to follow his manager's advice by throwing low and inside. It didn't work. In trying to force his mind away from the feared result, the pitcher could only fulfill the manager's negative advice. Spahn's pitch sailed wide and high in the strike zone, and Elston Howard swatted it over the fence for a home run.

If I asked you *not* to think of the color red for the next two minutes, would you be able to do it? Not really. Your mind would be drawn to red just by the suggestion of it. And the more you feared the consequences of disobeying my request, the more difficult it would be to keep your thoughts from gravitating to red. But if I asked you to think of the colors blue and yellow for two minutes, you could do it. And chances are, you wouldn't think of red because the negative suggestion has been replaced by a positive suggestion.

We use negative suggestion all the time. We say to others, "Don't be late," and what happens? We instruct our children, "Don't spill your milk," and what happens? "Don't, don't, don't"—but the words simply reinforce the possibility of the prohibited thought or action actually occurring. Often when we offer criticism to another person, we do it in a way that subconsciously encourages the negative behavior. And the more we harp on the negative, the greater the likelihood of its occurrence. But if you point to a desired behavior and spend time and energy talking about it, you increase the chances of that behavior happening.

Actually, the last thought you implant in your mind—or another's mind—will usually grow into the dominant behavior. Since fear peppers our thoughts with negative suggestions, fearful people usually produce fear-ridden behavior.

For example, everyone feels some sense of fear when encountering a new situation. Some people feel inhibited, crippled, and even paralyzed by fear in the situation, and they behave accordingly. Others move into the situation hopefully, focusing on the positives despite their fear, and they usually succeed. It's basically an attitude problem—our beliefs about ourselves and our outlook on life.

I'm not talking about a self-hype program of unrealistic positive thinking. I'm talking about steering our attitudes and thoughts *away* from fear-producing negatives and *toward* the hope-inspiring teachings of the Word of God. Believing that you must remain handcuffed and crippled by fear is a myth; it's a nonbiblical viewpoint. But believing that fear can be overcome and that you can move ahead in your life is a healthy, biblical viewpoint.

Do you talk like a victim?

As children we learned certain phrases that seemed innocent, but which have locked many of us in handcuffs as adults. Growing up believing these phrases has caused us to approach fear from a position of weakness. Here are some examples:

- I can't . . .
- That's a problem.
- I'll never . . .
- That's awful!
- I should . . .
- Why is life this way?
- If only . . .
- Life is a big struggle.
- What will I do?

By using phrases like these, you reinforce the control fear has over your life, and you remain handcuffed in a state of helplessness. You're usually not even aware of what you're doing to yourself. Every time you think or say one of these phrases, you subconsciously begin to believe it and fulfill it. You eventually talk yourself into believing that these phrases represent the truth. You become a victim of your fears. You fall prey to "victim phrases." Let's consider what happens when you believe and use victim phrases.

"I can't . . ." How many times a day do you say these words? Have you ever kept track? Do you realize these words are

prompted by fear? Think about it. Fear often hinders us from saying what we really feel and from being truthful.

When you say "I can't," you are saying you have no control over your life. A simple substitution of "I won't" or "I choose not to" at least gives you a choice, perhaps helping you eventually to say "I will" or "I choose to."

"That's a problem." People who see life's complications as problems or burdens are immersed in fear and hopelessness. Life is full of barriers and detours. But with every obstacle comes an opportunity to learn and grow—if you hold the right attitude. Using other phrases such as "That's a challenge," or "That's an opportunity for learning something new," leaves the door open for moving ahead.

"I'll never . . ." This victim phrase is the anchor of personal stagnation. It's the signal of unconditional surrender to fear. Saying instead, "I've never considered that before" or "I haven't tried it but I'm willing to try" opens the door to personal growth.

"That's awful." Sometimes this phrase is appropriate in view of the shocking, dire situations we often hear about in the day's news. But those events are extraordinary. In everyday experiences, "That's awful" is an inappropriate overreaction that is prompted by fear. Set a goal to eliminate its usage for life's ordinary problems. Instead, respond by saying "Let's see what we can do about this situation" or "I wonder how we can help at this time."

"I should . . ." This is one of the most controlling statements of all time. Every time you say "I should," you make yourself dependent upon something or someone else. You're at the mercy of whoever taught you the "should." "Should" sounds like an absolute, but it often isn't true or even necessary. Living up to a statement like "I should" is often difficult, and it can drain you emotionally because it generates guilt which then leads to fear. "I could" or "It might be nice to" or "I think I would like to" are healthier statements.

"Why is life this way?" This question is a normal response to the deep pains and sudden shocks of life. But there are those

who experience a major tragedy and choose to linger in the stages of shock, withdrawal, and confusion. They inappropriately use this question over and over again.

"Why is life this way?" and its companion statement, "Life isn't fair," are overused for the normal, minor upsets of everyday life. True, life *is* unpredictable and unfair. Life *isn't* always the way we want it to be. But our response to life is our choice, and the healthiest response is reflected in James 1:2-3: "Consider it wholly joyful, my brethren, whenever you are enveloped in or encounter trials of any sort, or fall into various temptations. Be assured and understand that the trial and proving of your faith bring out endurance and steadfastness and patience" (AMP). These verses encourage us to make up our minds to regard adversity as something to welcome or be glad about. *Joy in life is a choice*.

"*If only . . .*" This phrase anchors us to the past and imprisons us in bygone dreams. But the phrase "Next time" shows that we have given up our regrets, we have learned from past occurrences, we have put fear behind us, and we are getting on with our lives.

"*Life is a big struggle.*" This victim phrase reinforces the difficulties of life. Struggles can be and should be turned into adventures. Yes, it will take work. You may be stretched and you may feel uncomfortable. But this is the way to overcome your fear of life's difficulties.

"*What will I do?*"[3] This question is a cry of despair and fear of the future and the unknown. Instead say, "I don't know what I can do at this moment, but I know I can handle this. Thank God I don't have to face this issue by myself." Remember the encouraging words in Philippians 4:13: "I can do everything through him who gives me strength."

You've got to have hope

My pastor, Lloyd Ogilvie, once said, "If you harbor a fear, you become a landlord for a ghost." Fear will keep you chained to the very problem you are trying to kick out of your life. Fear is not the answer to the problems in your life; hope is the solution. Hope is allowing God's Spirit to set us free from our fears and draw us forward in our lives.

Hope is not blind optimism, it's realistic optimism. A person of hope is always aware of the struggles and difficulties of life, but he lives beyond them with a sense of potential and possibility. A person of hope doesn't just live for the possibilities of tomorrow, but sees the possibilities of today, even when his today is not going well. A person of hope doesn't just long for what he's missing in his life, but experiences what he has already received. A person of hope can say an emphatic *no* to fear and an energetic *yes* to life.

THREE

The Fear of Being Out of Control

Trying to control your own life imprisons you to the need to be in control.

Trusting in God's control results in a life of real freedom instead of a life of bondage.

"Fear not, for I have redeemed you; I have summoned you by name; you are mine." (Isa. 43:1)

Our raft was floating in the center of a swiftly flowing river that was about thirty feet wide. We steered the raft carefully around the boulders that jutted out of the water every few yards.

Then it happened. As we swept around a curve in the river, we saw another stream dead ahead that was pouring a torrent of water into our channel. We had been in control of our raft up to that point. But where the tributary merged with the main channel, the turbulence was more than we could handle. No effort at steering or slowing down worked. For several minutes, we were at the mercy of the two raging rivers, enduring the frightful experience of being completely out of control.

This fearful out-of-control feeling can envelop you anytime and anyplace. It can occur suddenly and unexpectedly—or so gradually you don't realize what's happening. One minute you're walking carefully on ice and snow, and suddenly you're out of control, flying through the air toward a painful encounter with the ground. Or you're sitting in a meeting that you have called for your own purposes, and gradually you are aware the meeting isn't going the way you wanted it to go. You have the sinking feeling that you're no longer in control. Or you're driving on the freeway and need to move into the right lane to make your exit. You signal and look for an opening in the traffic, but the other drivers are unwilling to let you change lanes. You helplessly watch your exit pass by, unable to control the situation.

Even though we express it in various ways, we all feel the need to be in control. For some, being in control is the driving, dominant force in their lives. For all of us, the amount of stress we experience is directly related to how much we feel we are in control of our lives and circumstances. And at the heart of this concern over control is fear. One of the greatest contributors to stress in men is the fear of feeling out of control. Though a woman may admit to this fear, a man rarely will because such a humbling confession adds to the tension.

One of the most common fears in life is the fear of losing control. The things we value most are the very things we feel we must have control over: power, prestige, a person, a job, status, and so forth. One who fears the loss of control becomes almost desperate in his attempts to stay in control.

Here are some facts about control and fear:

- If you are in a pressure-filled or undesirable situation *by choice*, you will often feel challenged or stimulated by it. But if that negative circumstance was thrust upon you or was not of your own choosing, it will be more stressful than challenging. Underlying the stress is the fear of being out of control.
- A man who quits his job feels like he retains control of his career; a man who is fired fears he has lost that control. A woman who chooses a job transfer to a new city feels she still has control of her situation; when she is told to transfer or lose her job, she feels out of control.
- When you can anticipate the consequences of a situation and foresee a bit of the future, you feel more in control. When the outcome of events in your life is unpredictable, the underlying stressful fear of being out of control can be present.

Controlled by fear

The controlling person makes it a point to be in control at all times. Slavish rigidity to rules—for himself and those around him—is the controller's life-style. The controller is only comfortable when he knows the outcome to everything, when the limits of life are clearly defined, and when there are no surprises.

Some extreme controllers constantly check and double-check to make sure nothing will go wrong. And when something *does* go haywire, the controller increases rigidity and attention to detail in order to bring life back under control. For most of these people, relationships take second place to order and routine. Details, structure, and lists become their bywords and their security.

Have you met anyone who comes across as domineering and controlling? If so, you've encountered someone motivated by fear. I've shared that truth with married couples sitting in my counseling office, especially when one partner is the overbearing, dominant type. When I initially raise the possibility of the controlling spouse being motivated by fear, I often hear disbelief in the response of the dominated partner. "Fear?" one wife retorted. "There's not a shred of fear in that man. He doesn't give others a chance. From the minute he meets them, he let's them know he's in charge. And anyone who shows any sign of controlling him is dominated immediately."

I responded to her by suggesting, "Perhaps his controlling nature is his way of never allowing anyone to get close enough to discover that he's afraid." She left my office with a new perspective on her domineering husband.

Controlling people strive for the appearance of being in control, but inwardly they live in fear. Many of them feel they cannot control their own feelings, so they attempt to control the way other people feel. They desperately want others to love them. But it's risky for controllers to give others the choice to love them (because they may choose *not* to!), so they demand love from others.

Control in disguise

For some controllers, every day is Halloween because they must constantly hide their fears behind acceptable social disguises.

These disguises are often ineffective and even harmful, but controllers feel they must mask their fears from others. Let's look at a few of these disguises.

The disguise of strength. In order to appear competent to others, fearful controllers try to appear strong. Physical strength and strength of character are admirable qualities, but they need to be genuine. Strength as a disguise often comes across as being overbearing and controlling, not genuine.

Once you portray this picture of strength, you lock yourself into this performance and can never be yourself. You actually allow others to control and dominate you by forcing you to look strong. In order to appear strong, you can never let down or back off. You always have to be up. It's also difficult to sit back, relax, and enjoy whatever success you have found. Your fears drive you always to stay ahead of others and set the pace.

This disguise of strength denies you the opportunity to enjoy others. How can you, since you are constantly comparing yourself to others in order to appear the strongest? What's worse, your show of strength doesn't help your fear disappear.

The disguise of love. Have you ever been smothered by an overly loving person? These individuals want the best for their loved ones. At first glance, they appear generous, and they openly share their concern for others.

But their love is really a mask hiding their fear of losing someone close to them. The fear of abandonment drives people to control their loved ones, but these efforts usually fail. And when controllers become aware of the lack of affection from their loved ones, few have the wisdom to back off and allow their loved ones to love them by choice. Unfortunately, controllers tend to be possessive, which further drives others away.

The disguise of procrastination. Have you ever been involved with a procrastinator—perhaps a friend, a family member, or even yourself? We tend to think of a procrastinator as someone who doesn't have all his ducks lined up in a row or whose mind is floating around the universe somewhere. But procrastinators are real, sane people whose behavior creates problems for themselves and others.

Procrastination is often only a symptom. Telling a procrastinator to "get with it" or to "get organized" is a monologue in futility. You need to understand why the procrastinator procrastinates. There are several reasons, and one of them is the desire to feel in control.

Many procrastinators feel an intense sense of independence. They procrastinate in order to demonstrate that no one can force them to do what they don't want to do. The procrastinator's behavior says, "You can't make me do it. I'm in control." It's the cry of the strong-willed adult! The procrastinator will do what he wants to do when he is good and ready, not when someone else tells him to do it.

The disguise of a martyr. Some people use the martyr approach to control others. They attempt to impose an excessive amount of responsibility on others through comments like:

- "Look at everything I've done for you."
- "You don't really care about anyone but yourself."
- "So this is how you thank me. I feel rejected."
- "You're not coming to visit me on vacation? I hope you enjoy yourself, even though I won't have a very good time."
- "It's your decision, but if you'd listen to me, you wouldn't have so many problems."
- "When you have children, I hope they treat you better than you've treated me."
- "You ought to be ashamed of the way you've been neglecting me."

Control in marriage

Some people want to make all the decisions in their marriages, and they demand to be in control of their spouses. When disagreements occur, power struggles develop. And the controlling partner uses numerous tactics to maintain control, including put-downs, intimidation, threats, a loud voice, and silence. The controller doesn't stop to consider the negative effect of his or

THE FEAR OF BEING OUT OF CONTROL

her behavior. In time, the affection of the controller's partner begins to diminish, even though he or she may be well provided for in other areas. As one person put it, "Who falls in love with his jailor?"

A controlling person is closed and unable to relate to his partner intimately. Controllers insist on being right, on winning, and on showing that others are wrong. They have great difficulty accepting blame. They profess expertise in too many areas and, because of their need to appear perfect, they cannot take criticism gracefully. Because of this behavior, they often feel unappreciated, especially by their spouses. Others give up in their attempts to love them since there is no real vulnerability.

Controlling people often feel alone and isolated even in their own marriages. But they are responsible for their condition. They have blocked off the positive emotional areas of their lives, and they have trod heavily on the feelings of others. They end up feeling hurt, wounded, rejected, and neglected. Do they admit their hurt? Not usually. Pain and hurt are not easy to admit, so these feelings often turn into anger, which feeds the tendency to control. [1]

To control or be controlled?

Some people take control in their lives because they fear the control, influence, or direction of others. Controlling behavior is the fear of trusting others. It's the fear of not being in charge of your own destiny or direction in life. It's the feeling that boasts, "I know what's best for me. I have all the knowledge and skill necessary to direct my life."

I wonder how controllers like these get along with God. I wonder how they learn to trust Jesus Christ as Savior. I wonder how they try to determine God's will for their lives (or maybe that question never enters their minds). I wonder how controllers handle the unexpected and uncontrollable crises of life and learn to view these upsets with a spiritual perspective. A controller cannot trust God because he fears the control of his life resting in anyone's hands but his own.

On the issue of control and fear as it relates to spiritual life, Lloyd Ogilvie states:

> Our need to be in charge of ourselves, others, and situations often makes our relationship with Christ life's biggest power struggle. We are reluctant to relinquish our control and allow Him to run our lives. We may believe in Him and be active in the church and Christian causes, but trusting Him as Lord of everything in life can be scary. Even though we pray about our challenges and problems, all too often what we really want is strength to accomplish what we've already decided is best for ourselves and others.
>
> Meanwhile, we press on with our own priorities and plans. We remain the scriptwriter, casting director, choreographer, and producer of the drama of our own lives, in which we are the star performer.[2]

Do you relate to what he said? Do you identify with any part of it? Many Christians do.

It's true that trusting another person—even God—is risky. Living by faith may be a new experience for you. But living a life of faith in Jesus Christ is far less risky than living a life of faith in ourselves. Trying to control your life imprisons you in the need to be in control. Trusting in His control leads to a life of freedom rather than a life of bondage.

You never were in total control! You're not in total control now! You never will be in total control! Why stay in bondage to the myth that you must be in control? There's a better way to live.

I'm not asking you to give up your life-style of control. All I'm asking you to do is to place the control of your life in Christ's hands for thirty days. Weigh the results, then decide which way you would prefer to live. It's really your choice.

Complete the following exercise in writing on a separate sheet of paper:

1. Describe the areas of your life in which you feel you must be in control. List statements or phrases you use to maintain control.

2. Brainstorm and identify the underlying fears that cause you to seek control.

3. For the next week, take several minutes each day to pray about your fears. Set up two chairs facing each other in an empty room. Sit in one of the chairs and pray aloud, talking to the empty chair as though God were sitting there. Describe for Him what you've written, and tell Him about your fears. Ask Him what you should do about your desire for control and your fears at this time. After the week is up, proceed with the rest of the items on this list.

4. Begin each day with prayer, admitting that you have a need (whether you feel it or not) to depend upon God rather than yourself for control in your life.

5. Identify one or two areas where you will give up some control each day. For example, you may decide to ask others for their opinions on issues and do what they suggest instead of asserting your opinion.

6. At the end of each day, write down your experiences for the day. Describe how you relinquished control, how you felt before and after, and what the benefits were or will be.

7. If you have difficulty with this assignment, go back to your fear. It's probably the main roadblock to experiencing Christ's control. Where did this fear originate? Who reinforced this fear? Take your fear to God each morning, talking aloud with Him, using the previously described empty-chair approach. Extend your hands upward, symbolically giving your fears to God. Imagine Him receiving your fears and offering to help you give up control in your life.

The fear of losing control weakens the most important relationship in your life: your relationship with Christ. It will keep you from experiencing the full joy and delight of the abundant life. Christ loves you and offers you His power. All He asks is that you accept His absolute control.

Surrender your will to His will and commit your total life—all that you are and have—to Him. God does want the best for you. It's clearly stated in His Word. Read it and you will discover He promises you His wisdom for your decisions, His supernatural strength for your challenges, and His love for your relationships. That's not a bad offer!

FOUR

The Fear of
Intimacy

Intimacy involves risking. We want to be close, but we are afraid of being close.

Intimacy eliminates the pain of loneliness and the pain of being strangers with one another.

Fill your life with the confidence of Jesus Christ.

"Do not be afraid, for I am with you." (Isa. 43:5)

The seminar participants filed into the room, talking and joking. As they settled into their chairs, a few noticed the statement that had been posted on the front wall. Soon most everybody had seen the statement, and many began to copy it down eagerly. When the seminar leader came in and began the session, he said nothing about the statement. After a while, one man in the group interrupted the leader by saying, "There's a statement on the wall."

The instructor turned, looked at the statement, and said, "Yes, there is," and continued his presentation.

Soon a few other curious hands began to slip up, and another participant asked, "Where is that statement from, and what does it mean?"

The instructor stopped and said, "That's an excellent question. How many of you were attracted to this statement?" Most of the group members raised their hands. "You asked me what the statement means, but I have another question. What does it mean to you? You have ten minutes to write your answer to my question." The statement on the wall provoked some furious writing and, later, excellent interaction on the topic of the fear of intimacy.

What was the statement this group couldn't wait to discuss?

Perhaps you've heard it before. It's from one of John Powell's books. It reads, "I'm afraid to tell you who I am because you might not like who I am and that's all I've got."

The meaning of intimacy

The fear of not being liked is a strong inhibitor of intimacy and closeness. On the one hand, we have a need for intimacy, but on the other hand, we often suffer from an immobilizing fear that resists this closeness. We want to be close, but we are afraid of being rejected, losing the love or respect of others, or discovering something we didn't wish to know about ourselves. We are afraid of being embarrassed.

To understand this fear, we have to understand intimacy, the source of our fear. Intimacy is the foundation for both love and friendship. It's a close emotional bond that involves mutual sharing and understanding.

Please note the word *mutual*. Each partner in an intimate relationship wants to know the other person's deepest dreams, wishes, concerns, hopes, and fears while at the same time being an open book himself. Intimacy leads to deep feelings of closeness, warmth, and trust. Intimacy eliminates the pain of loneliness and the pain of being strangers with one another. And there is no greater pain than being strangers in your own marriage. If you're going to have intimacy in your relationship, you must have the confidence to expose the private, vulnerable portion of your life. Intimacy means you cannot remain isolated from another.[1]

But sometimes intimacy hurts. Vulnerability carries with it the risk of being painfully real with another person. Mike Mason says:

> It is not intimacy itself, therefore, which is so distasteful and intimidating to the world, but rather the moral condemnation that comes with it. People crave closeness with one another, but are repelled by the sin that such closeness inevitably uncovers in themselves, the selfish motives that are unmasked, the pettiness that spills out, the monstrous

new image of self that emerges as it struggles so pitifully to have its own way.[2]

There are many who choose to be lonely to avoid the pain of developing intimacy. They are afraid of other people. It is an overwhelming task for them to reach out to others. Those who have experienced intimacy find it difficult to fathom this fear of closeness. Why would someone feel apprehensive about being emotionally close to another person?

One main reason is low self-esteem. If you constantly criticize yourself, you will probably fear that other people will follow your example and criticize you too. As one female client confessed, "When a man starts getting close, I run. I just know he's going to become critical of me. I'm enough of a critic of myself. I don't need his criticism." And the fear of seeing her own criticism come through another person keeps her blocked. If you want to be vulnerable to another person and experience love and closeness, you have to accept and love yourself.

Why women fear intimacy

There are several reasons women fear intimate relationships. One primary fear is the pain of rejection. Kimberly was a young divorcée who was attempting to make the adjustment back into single life. She complained:

I poured myself into that relationship for six years. I held nothing back, thinking my openness would make the marriage. It didn't. I feel abandoned and emotionally raped. I gave and he took. Then I got left behind. Why care that much? Why get that close? The closer you get, the more it hurts when they leave you. I was very close to my dad, and when he died at age forty-three it was like part of me was ripped away. And that happened just a year before my divorce. If you love them too much, they will kill you emotionally when they leave.

Yes, it does hurt when intimate relationships fall apart. But when there is *no* intimacy and closeness in a relationship, there is an *even greater chance* of a relationship dissolving! When you insulate yourself against others, you tend to bring about that which you fear the most—abandonment. The courage to run the risk of intimacy can bring tremendous fulfillment in life for both men and women.

Women also struggle with the fear of losing their identity in an intimate relationship with a man. Even though women tend to encourage and be more comfortable with intimacy than men, some women fear losing their sense of independence and autonomy if they get too close to their men.

We all need our own space, our privacy, and our separateness. That's normal. But some women are afraid a man's demands for closeness and sharing may become too energy-draining for them. They fear their men may begin to invade their lives too much. And in some cases, if a man is vulnerable and discloses his deepest feelings, both positive and negative, she fears he might be weak and unable to give her the care she desires.

Why men fear intimacy

It is rare to find a man who doesn't have some struggles with intimacy. Men love the benefits of intimacy, but often they are not committed to the work intimacy entails. Though few of them will admit it, most men fear intimacy, and this fear is reflected in the way they interact with their wives, families, and friends.

Why is it men avoid intimacy? Listen to a few of their responses, which reflect rationalizations rather than actual reasons:

"That's just the way men are. We aren't intimate the way women are. They may not like it, but that's just the way it is for us men."

"We don't know any differently. It's good enough for us.

We're satisfied with it. You can't really show us a better way."

"If you open up and share your feelings, others will take advantage of you. It's just not safe. It comes back to haunt you."

"You can't be macho and vulnerable at the same time. It just doesn't work, and I wouldn't know how to learn anyway."

"The main reason I can't be intimate is that when I try, my wife is the judge of whether or not I've shared a true feeling. I really *do* try to open up and get as close as she asks. But there's got to be a list of rules about feelings and closeness somewhere that only women know. From her perspective, I never get it right. So why try?"

"I don't think women want men to be all that vulnerable. They want someone they can depend on. When we do show feelings more, they don't know what to do with them. They can't handle them."

"I don't know whether or not I'm comfortable telling her everything. If I did something to make her mad, she'd use it against me. She's shared some things with her friends that I thought were only between the two of us. That hurt. I don't think women use good judgment when private discussions are concerned."

A major concern for men about intimacy with women is trust. Some men have had bad experiences after opening themselves up to the women in their lives. *Who* can be trusted? *When* can they be trusted? *What* can they be trusted with? Many men believe women perceive information differently, and they share in public what men see as only personal.

Another concern of men has its roots in the issue of control. When a man shares his personal thoughts and feelings in order to draw close to someone, he is potentially giving that person influence over him. That individual can use the information shared either *for* his welfare or *against* his welfare. It's risky. So withholding information helps a man retain a sense of control over his life and gain power over others.[3]

Many men fear losing this power over themselves and others. Research confirms that men withhold information about themselves in order to mislead others and often misrepresent themselves to others. Listen to what women have said about men and openness:

> "I really don't know how he feels."
> "He knows why he does what he does. But he doesn't tell me anything; he just does it."
> "Sometimes I think that's just the way men are."
> "I'm really puzzled about how to respond to him."
> "Apparently, men need to think about how they feel."
> "I'm not sure men know how they are supposed to feel."

But look at what men have said about themselves and openness:

> "I don't really know how I feel at times."
> "Who knows why I do what I do? It just happens."
> "That's just the way I am."
> "Honestly, I don't always know how to react."
> "I have to think about how I feel before I express it."
> "I don't know what I am supposed to feel."

Men often keep their thoughts and feelings a mystery in order to control the responses of others to them. But treating themselves as mysteries also helps men handle another fear they rarely admit to: the fear of really knowing themselves. When a man withholds information about himself from other people, he can avoid facing his own inconsistencies and inadequacies.

So avoiding intimacy is a controlling behavior that "helps" a man in two ways. First, it gives him the power over others that he associates with success in life. Second, it serves as protection against exposing his frailties to himself. Once again we see how fear can drive a person.

A growing body of research shows that men who live in isolation through a lack of intimacy suffer a definite decline in both physical and mental health. The absence of close, caring relationships is a source of stress for men. Elderly men have the highest suicide rate of all age groups, and stress is often the culprit. Heart attacks and cancer, the number one and number two killers of men, have also been tied to stress.

Cultivating social support is one of the best ways to handle the stress of life. Intimacy can modify or actually eliminate stressful circumstances in a man's life. Perhaps one way to override the fear of intimacy is to consider the health benefits—specifically stress reduction—intimacy can provide.

Fortunately, today many men are breaking out of their fears and discovering that sharing their problems with others creates an atmosphere for problem-solving. As men share their personal thoughts, feelings, and concerns with others, they realize the atmosphere of caring helps them explore alternatives and solutions to their problems more clearly. Intimacy is actually a means to a greater level of efficiency.[4]

Furthermore, when a man relates closely to others, he discovers a greater awareness of himself. Fears can be dissolved, and a healthy level of self-acceptance has an opportunity to develop.

Some men approach intimacy with reservations, saying, "If I do start to confront my fear of intimacy and open up, I need several things to keep myself going. I need to see there are more benefits in opening up than in staying closed. I need to see it's safe to open up. I don't want any negative value judgments about what I'm sharing. Nor do I want others telling me their opinion of what I think or feel inside. I need others to tell me it's OK to do this."

Men, be encouraged that others like you are hesitant about developing intimacy in relationships. It is a slow journey. It takes work and time. It involves a level of discomfort. It involves taking in more information about feelings. And it may involve participating in a small group of men who are willing to embark upon this same journey. But as one man who made the journey stated, "What was there to be afraid of in the first place? There are other things in life more terrifying than intimacy, and I've faced them. I guess I created my fear in the first place."

Three books can make a difference for a man who wants to develop intimacy: *The Secrets Men Keep*, by Dr. Ken Druck (Ballantine Books); *Men Have Feelings Too*, by G. Brian Jones (Victor Books); and *The McGill Report on Male Intimacy*, by Michael McGill (Harper and Row).

Why couples fear commitment

The fear of intimacy has impacted marriage statistics in our nation in the form of the fear of commitment. Many men and women are hesitant to take the step of commitment necessary for marriage.

It's true there is a need for being cautious in our commitments. But the fear of commitment causes some to hesitate and hesitate and hesitate, and the longer they wait, the greater the fear becomes.

When it comes down to making a relationship permanent through commitment, the subtle "what if" germ begins to invade our minds. "What if I'm attracted to someone else after I'm married?" "What if this isn't God's will for my life?" "What if I commit myself and the relationship fails?" "What if I commit myself and I get hurt?" Endless "what if" questions keep many couples from the commitment and intimacy that helps make a marriage strong.

Tim Timmons and Charlie Hedges talk about three of the major fears of commitment. First, there is the fear of giving love without receiving love in return. We all want to receive love in the same measure we give it. And in a marriage, giving without receiving is very painful.

Second, the fear of being used and taken advantage of is an inhibitor to commitment, especially after one partner gives personal information about himself.

Third, one of the most paralyzing fears preventing commitment is desertion. Desertion is the ultimate form of rejection. Anyone who has been jilted in the past always has the fear of desertion lurking in the back of his mind, blocking future commitments.[5]

Risk your way out of fear

What can you do about your fear of intimacy? Take a risk! Learn a new way to respond to the fear that causes you to shrink away from enriching, intimate relationships. Face your fear and override it.

The word *risk* may strike fear in your heart, but risking is the only way to grow. Taking a risk for intimacy means you will have to give up some false beliefs. For example, you must give up believing that intimacy always leads to hurt or that someone will take advantage of you. You may feel somewhat empty for the false beliefs you leave behind. Fill the void with the confidence that comes from your personal relationship with Jesus Christ. Fill it with the sufficiency of the Word of God. Fill it with the "fear not" promises of Scripture.

When you begin to build an intimate relationship, it is important to move slowly and ask the questions that come to mind. But at some point, you need to risk making a commitment in the relationship.

I like the illustration David Viscott gives concerning the risk of making a commitment. He calls it the point of no return and compares it to passing a car on a two-lane highway. When preparing to pass, you first assess the possibilities of passing, then you select the time and place, gather the momentum and power, and move out. When you hit the accelerator, you have taken a carefully calculated risk and have passed the point of no return. If you sense you're in danger after pulling out, hesitating and backing off will usually lead to an accident. But accelerating, sounding your horn, and creating a safe place for yourself is the best course.

Similarly, in intimacy you must carefully assess the relationship and make a commitment. True, once you pass the commitment point of no return, there is a greater possibility of being hurt. But you also have a greater possibility of succeeding in a relationship than you did before you risked the commitment.[6]

To help you conquer your fears and develop intimacy, complete the following exercise on a separate sheet of paper for one or more of your close relationships:

1. The type of relationship I would like with this person is . . .
2. The advantages of developing intimacy with this individual are . . .
3. What might happen if I commit myself to this person?
4. Does this person feel the same about our relationship as I do?
5. What are his/her thoughts about intimacy?
6. What do I want from this person?
7. Does he/she have the ability to give me what I want?
8. Who are the other people I have been close to in the past?
9. How did I benefit from being close to them?
10. What is the fear I may be experiencing now?
11. How much do I care about this person's feelings?
12. What are my feelings?
13. Does he/she care about my feelings?
14. What is my level of trust in this person?
15. What have I shared with this person about my feelings?
16. Two examples of sharing deep feelings with this person in the past are . . .
17. The results of sharing these feelings were . . .
18. What would happen if this person were not a part of my life?
19. Does this person need me?
20. What would I be most willing to share about myself with this person?
21. What would I be most hesitant to share with this person?
22. What is there about me that would disappoint or hurt this person if he/she knew?
23. What are five expectations I have for this person?
24. What are five expectations he/she has for me?
25. Topics we tend to avoid are . . .
26. Do I act real in this relationship? Why or why not?

27. How much is my self-esteem built upon this relationship?
28. We pray together when . . .
29. The indications that God is in this relationship are . . .
30. The way I pray for this person is . . .
31. The way I have been praying for this relationship is . . .
32. What it will take for me to risk greater openness and intimacy in this relationship now is . . .
33. What I intend to do now with this relationship is . . .[7]

FIVE

The Fear of Rejection

Many of us live with ghosts of rejection. The fear of rejection consumes us.

It causes us to compromise who we really are.

But there is an ultimate source of acceptance, One who will fulfill all of our needs.

"But God, who is rich in mercy, out of the great love with which he loved us, . . . made us alive together with Christ. . . . For we are his work-manship, created in Christ Jesus for good works." (Eph. 2:4-5, 10, RSV)

"I don't want you on my team."

"I don't like you."

"I don't love you."

"I'm sorry, but we can't use your services."

"You just won't work out in our organization."

"Sorry, but we will not accept your article."

"You have to change. You're just not good enough the way you are."

Simple statements, short statements. But they all carry a great amount of pain. Statements like these hurt us no matter how much we say, "It doesn't matter." Being rejected hurts, so we all fear rejection. And each time we experience rejection, our fear intensifies. The fear of rejection tempts us to deny who we really are in order to succeed in our quest for acceptance and love.

Our bout with rejection usually begins in childhood, as Lloyd Ogilvie describes:

> For some it might have begun with an aching suspicion that their parents favored one sibling over another. Others, who didn't battle sibling rivalry, still did not experience the esteem-building affirmation of their parents.
>
> Many felt rejection when they did not excel in athletics.

There was intense anxiety when they lined up for the choosing of teams for a ball game. It was painful to be the last one chosen or not to be chosen at all. Or think of the times we were not accepted by the "in" group of kids in the neighborhood or at school. I can remember my first infatuation and the pain of discovering that my "heartthrob" didn't even know I existed.

Who can forget the longing to be popular? Think of the times we stood with wallflower anticipation at a school dance or wondered if we would have a date for the prom.

Added to all this was the fear of failure in school and the sense of rejection when we didn't quite measure up. Pressure from parents or competition from our peers made us equate grades with our value as persons. A poor grade was like a rejection slip from life.[1]

Why do we feel rejected?

Some of us are especially sensitive to any hint of rejection. And because of this tendency, rejection is seen in statements and actions when it isn't even there. We live with the ghosts of rejection. Every rejection we've experienced in the past causes us to be overly sensitive to being rejected in the present. The pain of previous rejections stays with us; it haunts us.

Judy was a young woman who looked like she was afraid of rejection. When she came into the room, her eyes pleaded, "Accept me; tell me I'm all right." Starving for approval and overly sensitive to any look or remark that hinted of nonacceptance, Judy was certain that others did not want her. She read nonexistent rejection into neutral or even positive conversation. She *expected* to be rejected. Unfortunately, even when others were friendly and accepting, she was suspicious of them. In her words, "If I trust them, who's to say it's not some trick on their part. They'll just reject me when I'm not looking, and because I trusted them, it will hurt even worse!" Judy's fear of rejection was consuming her.

Others who fear rejection come from childhood homes where

they were treated as unacceptable, unwanted burdens. Feelings of rejection in childhood can result from the presence of derogatory statements or the absence of physical or verbal affirmation. When a person is rejected as a child, he is more sensitive to hurt as an adult.

Ted grew up in a home where everybody was work-oriented and very busy. There was no emotional closeness, physical affection, or interest shown to the children. Ted's parents were busy with their own lives and showed very little interest in Ted and his accomplishments at school. In his teen years, Ted began to wonder why his family wasn't close to him and why no one took much interest in him. He pondered what it was about him his parents didn't like. They weren't mean or abusive to him. They were polite and courteous, but sterile in their responses. Ted said:

> I never could understand why they were so distant. We were together as a family, but it felt like we were miles apart. And then I began to wonder if there was something wrong with me. I felt like I was a burden even though they always provided for me. They never said I was a burden— but I felt that way.
>
> Because of my childhood experience, I've always been fairly cautious about getting close to someone. Maybe there is something wrong with me, and I just can't see it. Sometimes I have daydreams and night dreams about others rejecting me. In my relationships with women, I'm very cautious about getting involved. I'm afraid they will do what my parents did—ignore me. To me, being ignored hurts the same as someone telling me, "You stink. You're no good. I don't like you, and I don't want you." My folks never said those words exactly, but their actions made me feel as though they had.
>
> If I meet a woman I'm interested in, I begin to wonder, "Will she really like me or want me?" I would rather wait for a woman to show an interest in me and pursue me. That's safer. I don't like to pursue them because if they

turn me down, I feel like I've lost a part of who I am. Rejection brings up all those adolescent feelings I had at home. I wish I wasn't this cautious.

Everybody feels rejected sometimes

What part does past or present rejection play in our lives?

Any rejection we feel stirs up the embers of fear that slowly burn within us. Every rejection we experience is like another piece of coal that is fed to the flames.

Everyone experiences this kind of pain in life. Even Jesus experienced rejection. Isaiah the prophet told of Christ's rejection when he said, "He was despised and rejected by men, a man of sorrows, and familiar with suffering" (Isa. 53:3). He was rejected by the leaders of Israel and denied and betrayed by others.

You can feel rejection whether you are single or married. And perhaps rejection from a marriage partner is one of life's ultimate hurts. The closer you are to someone, the more it hurts when they show disapproval or say, "I don't want you anymore."

Are you aware of your own feelings of rejection? How deep are they? Take a moment to think about your own feelings of rejection by answering these questions:

- When in your life have you been rejected?
- Describe your feelings of being rejected.
- How have these rejections affected you?
- In what way do you reject yourself?

Did that last question throw you? If you've experienced enough rejection in our life, your fear of being rejected again will cause you to behave in ways that bring about rejection. And many people are so down on themselves that they are their own worst enemies. They put themselves down, degrade themselves, dump on themselves, and rarely give themselves the benefit of the doubt. And since they don't like themselves, they project a negative picture of themselves to others. They operate on the false belief that since they don't like themselves, no one else could possibly like them either.

Those who live with the fear of rejection are sometimes described by others as being overly sensitive, overly cautious, or overly starved for acceptance. You've met people like this, and so have I. And at times in our lives, perhaps we've been there too.

Consider how the fear of rejection causes us to respond to life. Mary was a very sensitive person who had experienced rejection in her childhood home and in some of her relationships with men. As we talked together, Mary revealed the extent of her feelings:

> I don't like the way I am. I know I'm overly sensitive. When I made the appointment with you, I even wondered if you would accept me as a client. Then when I arrived this morning and you were three minutes late for my appointment, those old feelings of rejection began to climb to the surface. It wasn't you but my own sensitivity. I feel that way whenever someone changes plans with me or disagrees with what I think or want. Anytime someone doesn't go along with what I want, I begin to feel rejected. And then I get angry inside.
>
> When I am dating a man and I care for him, I'm even more sensitive to any sign of rejection. But when I feel rejected, I come on too strong and demand love and acceptance in some way. And that chases him right out the door! When that happens, I feel terrible. And I know I caused the rejection. But I don't know what to do!
>
> That's not the only way I respond to my fear of rejection. Sometimes I feel real inhibited with a man, so I withdraw. I'm afraid of exposing my true self and being rejected. But my withdrawal also brings on rejection because he sees me as a real dud. I can't let him know that I care for him and crave his attention and acceptance. So I don't get it. And once again, I get mad! It's almost like I'm caught in a vicious cycle. But I don't know how to get out of it!

Mary's right: It *is* a vicious cycle. And it's common. When a person lives with the fear of rejection, he has an excessive need for acceptance by others. But he behaves in such a way that prevents him from experiencing acceptance. He is either so overly timid, restrained, and closed that no one can get in, or so demanding that he drives others away. In either case, he is rejected because most people do not respond well to either his withdrawal or his demands.

Feelings of rejection breed anger and even rage, but angry feelings are not usually expressed directly since they would bring about more rejection. And so the fear intensifies, which causes the person to need even more acceptance and reassurance, which causes him to respond at even deeper levels of withdrawal or demand. The vicious cycle continues and continues. The same protective devices we created to exorcise rejection from our lives only create more fear and rejection.

Addicted to approval

The fear of rejection can cause us to compromise who we really are. As Esau sold his birthright for a bowl of lentil stew, so we forfeit our identity in order to gain the approval of others. Some people even become approval addicts. Underneath their fear of rejection is the misbelief that it is terrible and tragic if someone disapproves of them. And underlying this misbelief is the faulty reasoning, "If someone disapproves of me, there must be something wrong with me, and this defect will cause others to disapprove of me as well."

There is a high price to pay for addiction to the approval and acceptance of others. The price tag includes an extreme vulnerability to the whims and subjective opinions of the people around you. Others can take advantage of your vulnerability and mistreat you, which leads to additional rejection.

Another false belief held by approval addicts is, "If I am accepted by others and not rejected, I will be satisfied and happy, and my life will be fulfilled." But no experience of approval leads to permanent satisfaction. Every acceptance "fix" soon wears off, and the fear of rejection returns with a stronger craving for approval.

In reality, we all have varied needs for approval, and the intensity of these needs fluctuates. You may handle some rejections quite well, but some—especially rejection from those who are significant to you—can crush and devastate you. Don't be fooled into thinking that you can gain the approval of everyone.

The fear of rejection causes us to become people-pleasers, to call attention to ourselves, or to act inappropriately or awkwardly. And in so doing we set ourselves up for rejection. We become a pawn to the need that drives us toward others. We develop anxiety about confronting people. We fear expressing an unpopular or different idea that could elicit a conflict of opinion.

The people-pleaser response—also called a compliance compulsion—is very prevalent. I see this pattern in my counseling practice more and more, especially in wives. Perhaps this accounts for the popularity of a recent book entitled *The Pleasers* by Kevin Leman.

For people who please, the anger and rage that build up from repeated compromises and rejections finally seek expression. Many people-pleasers who come to me realize there must be a better way to respond to rejection than they now practice.

The people-pleaser response is often seen in the "good person." This individual acts friendly, is compliant, and gives out favors left and right in order to insure acceptance. But the fulfillment of his own needs is denied since a good person seeking acceptance has little time left for himself.

Those fearing rejection may also appear shy, timid, or ill at ease around others. These people seem to dodge close relationships, some of them commenting, "Who needs other people?" But this attitude is often translated, "I'm afraid of being rejected." Others may appear cool, aloof, superior, distant, or indifferent.

The shy person subconsciously expects to be rejected when reaching out. His behavior says, "Those people out there are to be feared. They could hurt me. They may not like me. Who would be interested in me? I'm not very sharp, and I can't converse like others. Anyway, a person who would like me must have something wrong with them. They wouldn't be worth getting involved with anyway. I'm not going to say anything. I'll just make a jerk of myself." Did you notice the negative self-talk? Unfortunately, every crippling statement becomes a self-fulfilling prophecy.

There are a number of false beliefs shy people hold onto as the basis for their fear of rejection. Those who withdraw and appear shy often give these reasons for their life-styles:

- "I must make a good, positive first impression. If I don't, they will never like me or accept me." (The hesitancy behind this belief may make the initial impression a disaster!)
- "I must be clear and articulate. Otherwise, I shouldn't even try to express myself."
- "I must know how to initiate conversation with others in all situations."
- "I need to have the perfect opening line." (This belief is sure to distract a person from ever opening his mouth. There *is* no perfect opening line!)
- "I must be comfortable and fully at ease before I engage others in conversation. Otherwise, they will notice my discomfort and reject me."

Another misbelief shy people hold has been called "the myth of the rescuer." Some people hope that somewhere in the world there is an individual who will rescue them from their relationships, take care of them, and protect them from all rejection. But, of course, the myth of the rescuer is exactly that—a myth.[2]

Dealing with your fear of rejection

We've identified the problem all right, but by now you're probably asking, "What do I do about my fear of rejection?"

There *is* hope. Your fear of rejection can diminish and ultimately vanish. It *is* possible, especially when your hope is in the person of Jesus Christ. That's how we begin to overcome both the effects of rejection and the fear of rejection. We need to tap into the ultimate source of acceptance, who will fulfill all of our needs.

Do you realize how much God accepts you? God sees you as worthy of the precious blood of His Son. Consider the following verses that tell us so:

● "Do you not know that your body is a temple of the Holy Spirit, who is in you, whom you have received from God? You are not your own; you were bought at a price. Therefore honor God with your body" (1 Cor. 6:19-20).

● "For you know that it was not with perishable things such as silver or gold that you were redeemed from the empty way of life handed down to you from your forefathers, but with the precious blood of Christ, a lamb without blemish or defect" (1 Pet. 1:18-19).

● "And they sang a new song [to the Lamb]: 'You are worthy to take the scroll and to open its seals, because you were slain, and with your blood you purchased men for God from every tribe and language and people and nation'" (Rev. 5:9).

Furthermore, God knows you through and through! He is fully aware of you:

● "And the Lord said to Moses, 'I . . . am pleased with you and I know you by name'" (Exod. 33:17).

● "Before I formed you in the womb I knew you, before you were born I set you apart" (Jer. 1:5).

● "I am the good shepherd; I know my sheep and my sheep know me . . . and I lay down my life for the sheep. . . . My sheep listen to my voice; I know them . . . and they shall never perish" (John 10:14-15, 27-28).

Dr. James Packer writes: "There is tremendous relief in knowing that His love to me is utterly realistic, based at every point on prior knowledge of the worst about me, so that no discovery now can disillusion him about me, in the way I am so often disillusioned about myself, and quench His determination to bless me. . . . He wants me as His friend, and desires to be my friend, and has given His Son to die for me in order to realize this purpose."[3]

The times in our lives when we are at peace with ourselves, not bound by the past, are the times we feel as though we belong. We feel wanted, desired, accepted, and enjoyed. We feel worthy: "I count; I'm good." We also feel competent: "I can do it." These feelings are essential because they give us our sense of identity.

But our times of feeling complete may be all too infrequent. We must continually remember our roots, our heritage. We are created in the image of God. He wants His work to be complete in us. When we relate to His Son Jesus Christ by faith, we have the potential for inner wholeness. (See Colossians 2:10.)

Joseph Cooke offers further encouragement:

> This, then, is the wonder of the Christian message: that God is this kind of God; that He loves me with a love that is not turned off by my sins, my failures, my inadequacies, my insignificance. I am not a stranger in a terrifying universe. I am not an anomalous disease crawling on the face of an insignificant speck in the vast emptiness of space. I am not a nameless insect waiting to be crushed by an impersonal boot. I am not a miserable offender cowering under the glare of an angry deity. I am a man beloved by God Himself. I have touched the very heart of the universe, and have found His name to be love. And that love has reached me, not because I have merited God's favor, not because I have anything to boast about, but because of what He is, and because of what Christ has done for me in the Father's name. And I can believe this about God (and therefore about myself) because Christ has come from the Father, and has revealed by His teaching, by His life, by His death, by His very person that this is what God is like: He is "full of grace."[4]

If you fear rejection, you have a selective memory that needs to be switched to a new channel. Yes, it's true you have been rejected by others in the past. But what about the times you *have* been accepted? They are there! Believe it! Look for them! Moses had to remind the children of Israel about the times God led them. We too need to be called back to positive memories.

Another step in dealing with your fear of rejection is to identify and list your misbeliefs about acceptance and rejection. Become aware of both the blatant and subtle messages—like those mentioned earlier in this chapter—that are directing your responses in life.

Then, before focusing on your fear of rejection from others, consider the ways you reject yourself. It could be that you make rejecting statements about yourself. If so, train yourself to counter each rejecting statement with three positive, affirming statements. It could be that you see yourself responding to others in such a way that they *will* reject you. Each time you see yourself responding in a hesitant or inadequate manner, imagine yourself in a healthy, positive manner. How you think about yourself, see yourself, and talk about yourself determines what happens in your life.

In southern Africa, the Babemba tribe has a fascinating procedure for combatting feelings of rejection. Each person in the tribe who acts irresponsibly or unjustly is taken alone to the center of the village. Everyone in the village stops work and gathers in a large circle around the accused. In turn, each person in the tribe—regardless of age—speaks to the individual, recounting aloud the good things he has done in his lifetime. All the positive incidents in the person's life, plus his good attributes, strengths, and kindnesses, are recalled with accuracy and detail. Not one word about his irresponsible or antisocial behavior is shared.

The ceremony, which sometimes lasts several days, isn't complete until every positive expression has been given by those assembled. At the conclusion of the ceremony, the person is welcomed back into the tribe. Can you imagine the flood of feelings this person experiences during the tribe's welcome? Can you imagine the extent of acceptance he realizes? Can you imagine how you would feel if a group of people affirmed you in this way?

But what about you? Do you accept yourself in that way? Do you surround yourself with affirming and encouraging responses? God does! He has surrounded you with more responses than you can ever hear. And one of His responses, repeated again and again in Scripture, is "Fear not!" Stop persecuting yourself and prosecuting yourself by fearing rejection. Accept yourself and relish God's acceptance.

When rejection happens

Remember: When someone does respond to you in a rejecting manner, it may be that he or she is having a bad day. Or perhaps that person has misinterpreted your response—or is just a critical, hurting person! It may be somebody else's problem. Or maybe nobody is at fault; the incident that made you feel rejected just happened for some unexplained reason. Being rejected doesn't necessarily mean you have done or said something wrong.

If someone shares a valid criticism with you, focus on the criticism and don't interpret it as a rejection. If the criticism is valid, learn and grow from it. Every person is imperfect and inadequate, and we all have room to grow.

If you make a mistake and are afraid of being rejected, don't anticipate being rejected ahead of time. Balance your feelings by focusing on the numerous times you *were* successful. See your small mistake in the context of the positive side of your life.

Criticism and rejection from others can upset you only to the extent that you believe the response of the other person. You can let it linger and destroy you, or you can move ahead. Yes, rejection does hurt, and it's uncomfortable. But avoid the hippopotamus response—don't wallow in your feelings of rejection. Refuse to believe that one rejection will lead to others or that your world is falling apart. Instead, take charge of the situation when it occurs, and turn the negative into a positive by responding to it with courage.

When you are rejected, keep in mind that other people have neither the right nor the ability to judge your value and worth as a person. Don't allow the negative responses of others to determine your value. People are not the experts on your worth; God is. I like what Dr. David Burns says about approval and disapproval: "It's a fact that approval *feels* good. There's nothing wrong with that: it's natural and healthy. It is also a fact that disapproval and rejection usually taste bitter and unpleasant. This is human and understandable. But you are swimming in deep, turbulent waters if you continue to believe that approval and disapproval are the proper and ultimate yardsticks with which to measure your worth."[5]

When you live with the fear of rejection, you live with assumptions based on emotions. Your emotions tell you what to believe about events and relationships. They tell you that you will be rejected and that you *are* rejected. Counter these feelings with actual facts. Unless you behave in a way that causes you to be rejected, most of the time you won't be rejected. But when you are rejected, don't assume that you are at fault.

I have felt rejection. I have felt the rejection of someone not liking my speaking, my writing, or my counseling. I have had my ideas rejected, and I have been personally rejected by other people. I don't like it. In fact, it's so uncomfortable to feel rejected, I've often wondered why anyone would want to live with the fear of rejection.

When you and I feel rejected, we need to remember who accepts us. The words of Amy Carmichael, a missionary to India a few generations ago, have encouraged me:

> Sometimes circumstances are so that we must be misunderstood, we cannot defend ourselves, we lie open to blame, and yet we may know ourselves clear before God and man in that particular matter. The King of our lives knows! If we are to blame, it cannot be hidden from Him. And when we are unjustly criticized or condemned, He understands. In

either case, He wants to join with us in a majority opinion of two that no matter what has happened, we have a bright future and can press on without dreading the next rejection.[6]

Could I make one final suggestion? To confront and defeat the fear of rejection, dwell upon a positive thought. A few lines our pastor, Lloyd Ogilvie, uses have been very helpful to many. Speak these words aloud every morning and evening for the next month. You will be amazed at the effect: "Secure in God's love, I will not surrender my self-worth to the opinions and judgments of others. When I am rejected, I will not retaliate; when I am hurt, I will allow God to heal me. And knowing the pain of rejection, I will seek to love those who suffer from its anguish."[7]

SIX

The Fear of
Loving Again

The trauma of a lost love is one of life's most
painful hurts.

The fear of loving again is one of life's greatest
fears.

Fear freezes your life in place.

*"For I know the plans I have for you, says the
Lord, plans for welfare and not for evil, to give
you a future and a hope."* (Jer. 29:11, RSV)

Heartbreak, disappointment, loneliness, numbness—these are words that describe those who have experienced broken friendships, broken engagements, and broken marriages. Furthermore, every survivor of a broken relationship is haunted by a residue of fear about future relationships. Some people face their breakups squarely, learn from them, override their fears, and grow to trust and love again. But others allow their emotional wounds to remain perpetually open; they give in to their fears by withdrawing from intimate relationships. The trauma of love lost is one of life's most painful hurts, and the fear of loving again is one of life's greatest fears.

When you have trusted another person with your feelings of love and affection, and the relationship ends, your life seems to come to a standstill for awhile. Usually the first love lost is the most painful. Some of the men and women who hurt the most are those who are still deeply attached to their former spouses or fiancées and want the relationship to be restored. They feel desperate, totally out of control, and willing to do almost anything to keep their partners. But they have no control over their loved ones' decisions.

Being out of control in any situation is fearful, but having no control over a broken relationship is intensely fearful. Watching your loved one slip away without any recourse leaves you feeling empty and impotent. You feel like you're unraveling emotionally.

Once your intimate relationship ends, a part of you wants to try again with a new relationship. But another part of you says, "Don't! It isn't worth the risk!" You're afraid the past will recur and your new relationship will also end in a painful breakup. Or you're afraid you will always feel the loss and pain of your previous breakup and never be able to reach out and love again. This fear is intensified whenever you relive the breakup. Every time the painful scenario replays in your memory, the emotional sledgehammer crashes down on you again. With some this fear can bring on panic attacks. I've even heard people say they thought they were going crazy during this phase.

The fear of reliving the past paralyzes the normal process of building a new relationship. This fear creates a hesitancy to invest energy, love, and transparency in a new love interest. Many people who are afraid to move ahead in a new relationship are also afraid to remain behind without anyone to love. They feel trapped between the fear of loving again and the fear of never being loved again.

Other emotions feed the fear of loving again. One of them is guilt—the feeling that we have failed ourselves, our ideals, our Lord, or the other person. This guilt may exist whether you were the *rejected* person or the *rejecting* person. Unresolved guilt damages self-esteem, and low self-esteem produces greater fear. If you feel guilty about a broken relationship, it's important to identify whether the feelings are real (from breaking a commitment or acting irresponsibly toward another) or imagined (from taking responsibility for something that was not really your responsibility).

Another emotional response to a broken relationship is anger. This strong feeling of irritation or displeasure occurs when we have been hurt, when we are afraid, or when we are frustrated.

When anger continues, it turns into resentment. Anger and resentment often give people a temporary sense of control or power that feels much more comfortable than the insecurity of fear. Fear generates anger, but eventually anger leads back to fear. The fear you're trying to overcome may be lurking just beneath the surface. It hasn't gone away; it's just camouflaged.

Many people have found relief from anger or resentment in broken relationships by writing a letter—which is never sent—to the other person. Once the letter is written, the writer goes into a room by himself and arranges two chairs facing one another. He sits in one chair and places in the other a sheet of paper with the name of the other person written on it. Then he reads the letter aloud as though the other person were actually sitting there. Consider this method. It's a healthy way of releasing anger and resentment.

The crisis of a lost love

Depending on the intensity of the relationship, most breakups result in a form of personal crisis. Webster defines *crisis* as "a crucial time" and "a turning point." The term describes your inner responses to your outward circumstances. When you experience a relationship crisis, it seems as though everything is on the line. You often feel numb, empty, and disoriented. Your entire life is overshadowed by the breakup.

In all crises, there are certain predictable stages everyone goes through to recover from the devastation. These stages constitute the normal and healthy process of recovery. This is your time of healing. If the healing is complete, you may have an emotional scar or two, but you will be able to function well in the future. If you do not allow the healing process to take place, your emotional wounds will continue to fester painfully, blocking future relationships.

There are usually six stages you will go through when a love relationship falls apart. Your pain will be the greatest during the first three stages. But as you move through each stage, the intensity of your pain will diminish. The farther along the path you proceed, the less fear you will experience.

Some of these stages overlap, and you may move back and forth between them for a while. This is quite normal. It's a part of the healing process. The worst thing that can happen is to get stuck in one of the stages and not complete the process.

Stage One: Shock. When you first lose a love relationship, you feel dumbfounded and overwhelmed by shock. Even when the breakup or divorce has been anticipated, the reality of it has a unique effect. Some people are unable to carry on their day-to-day activities; even eating and sleeping are a chore. You live by your feelings at this stage.

Whether or not you can identify it, you will experience an intense fear of being alone or of being abandoned forever. But you need to experience these feelings in order to move through the healing process. At this stage, you need to have other people around you, whether or not you feel like having them around. Just the presence of another person can help ease the fear of loneliness.

Stage Two: Grief. The grief stage may be extensive since it includes mourning the loss of what you shared together and what you *could have* shared together. During this time the anger mentioned earlier may be felt and expressed. You may be angry at yourself, at God, and at others who don't understand your grief. You may become depressed during this stage about the broken relationship behind you and the hopelessness of relationships in the future.

Stage Three: Blame. Feelings of blame, accompanied by anger, may be held toward your former spouse, fiancée, or dating partner—or even toward yourself. Your behavior during this stage may surprise you as you attempt to rid yourself of these feelings. Your actions may not seem to fit your past patterns. You may engage in compulsive behaviors such as shopping or eating binges, alcohol abuse, or even promiscuity. It's not unusual for people to make poor decisions at this stage. Fears of rejection, isolation, or personal inadequacy prompt some people to act contrary to their own value systems.

Jim was a thirty-five-year-old man whose wife divorced him to marry her employer. Jim was devastated by the divorce, but gradually he began to date again. However, he was quite unsuccessful in his new relationships. As we talked about the crisis stages in his situation, he realized he might be stuck in this third stage. One day Jim explained:

> I guess I'm still angry at my wife for leaving me. But there's no way I can make her pay for what she did to me, and I can't take my anger out on her. So that's probably why these new relationships aren't working out. I like the women I date, but I don't treat them well. I get angry at them, and I'm often rude. That's just not me! I guess I'm trying to get back at my wife by taking my anger out on these other women. And that isn't good for them or for me. I guess I try to hurt them first because I'm afraid they may hurt me like my wife did. And I don't ever want to be hurt like that again!

Fortunately Jim had the insight to figure out what he was doing, and eventually he moved out of this stage.

Stage Four: Good-bye. This stage is often difficult to face. It involves saying good-bye. This is when you finally admit to yourself, "The relationship is over; this person is out of my life, and I have to go on." I've seen numerous people get stuck on the threshold of this stage, sometimes for more than a year. Some of them seem to move ahead, yet three weeks later they are asking the same questions and making the same statements about a reconciliation that will never happen. They are unwilling to say the final good-bye.

Stage Five: Rebuilding and *Stage Six: Resolution*. At these stages, you are finally able to talk about the future with a sense of hope. You have just about completed your detachment from the other person, hopefully without lingering fears. Healthy new attachments may occur at this time.

We need to remember, however, that there are three possible outcomes of a relationship crisis: a change for the better; a change for the worse; or a return to the previous level of living. At the outset of the crisis, it is almost impossible to conceive of things changing for the better, especially if you are the one who was rejected. In the latter stages of the crisis, you may be able to see glimmers of possibility for positive change. Your judgments and decisions during this turning point in your life will make the difference in the outcome—positive or negative.

The desired outcome of the crisis points in your life, of course, is growth and a change for the better. What kind of growth or change can you expect? Consider the words of Dr. Lloyd Ogilvie as he talks about what he has discovered from the valleys of his life:

> First, it has been in the valleys of waiting for answers to my prayers that I have made the greatest strides in growing in the Lord's grace.
>
> Second, it's usually in retrospect, after the strenuous period is over, that I can look back with gratitude for what I've received of the Lord Himself. I wouldn't trade the deeper trust and confidence I experienced from the valley for a smooth and trouble-free life.
>
> Third, I long to be able to remember what the tough times provide in my relationship with the Lord, so that when new valleys occur, my first reaction will be to thank and praise the Lord in advance for what is going to happen in and through me as a result of what happens to me. I really want my first thought to be, "Lord, I know You didn't send this, but You have allowed it and will use it as a part of working all things together for good. I trust you completely, Lord."[1]

Don't expect to have this insight during the initial three stages of your crisis. You must work through those early, difficult feelings. But in time the attitude Dr. Ogilvie describes is genuinely possible.

Overcoming your relationship crisis

When you are experiencing the pain and fear of a relationship crisis, you can take several steps to ease your feelings and lead to a change for the better in your life. Let's consider them one by one:

1. Identify your feelings. When a close relationship is severed, you must face your feelings straight on. Describe your feelings in writing, working either alone or with a friend. Take plenty of time for this exercise and include as much detail as you possibly can remember. Keep your description handy, and whenever you find your mind drifting back to the breakup, take out your written account and ask yourself the following questions:

● Are there any new thoughts I need to write down?
● What will I learn by rereading the account?
● What will it do for me to reread this account?
● What am I trying to change by rereading this account?
● Right now my greatest fear is . . .

These questions may help you interrupt your tendency to endlessly recount the negative details and feelings of your crisis. I'm not suggesting you stop thinking about your experience. But all too often we only focus on the painful statements or actions and berate ourselves too much in the process.

2. Read the Scriptures. There are numerous passages in God's Word that will comfort you during a time of intense loss. You may want to write out several of them and have them available to read when you feel fearful, angry, or depressed. Here are some passages helpful to me:

● "Nehemiah said, 'Go and enjoy choice food and sweet drinks, and send some to those who have nothing prepared. This day is sacred to our Lord. Do not grieve, for the joy of the Lord is your strength'" (Neh. 8:10).
● "Even though I walk through the valley of the shadow of death, I will fear no evil, for you are with me; your rod and your staff, they comfort me" (Ps. 23:4).
● "But I trust in you, O Lord; I say, 'You are my God'" (Ps. 31:14).

- "You will keep in perfect peace him whose mind is steadfast, because he trusts in you" (Isa. 26:3).
- "He will be the sure foundation for your times, a rich store of salvation and wisdom and knowledge; the fear of the Lord is the key to this treasure" (Isa. 33:6).
- "'For I know the plans I have for you,' declares the Lord, 'plans to prosper you and not to harm you, plans to give you hope and a future'" (Jer. 29:11).

3. Communicate with others. Share your feelings, concerns, and especially your fears with a trusted friend. Be sure to tell your friend whether you want him or her just to listen to you or to give you verbal comfort and advice. Sometimes your friends don't really know what you need or want unless you tell them.

4. Find some diversions. During your recovery from a crisis, you need some activities to keep your mind and hands occupied. You need to get involved in a healthy diversion even if you don't feel like doing it. Let your friends know what you enjoy doing so they can assist you in the process of being distracted from your feelings and fears.

I have a number of clients who have found great comfort in their pets. In fact, male heart attack victims who own pets have a much lower mortality rate than those who don't. Pets make great listeners, and they usually don't interrupt.[2]

Keeping your thoughts in check

One of the most significant factors in your recovery and freedom from crippling fears is the control of your thought life. During a crisis, our thoughts tend to run rampant. We are the victims of automatic thoughts from time to time that just pop into our minds without any conscious regard on our part. And when our focus is on the rejection and pain of disintegrated relationships, the unbidden thoughts that come to mind are not usually productive. You may tend to overgeneralize in your thinking, resort to "all or nothing" thinking, reject positive thoughts, jump to conclusions, use "should" or "ought" statements, or employ emotional reasoning or labels.

No matter what type of thinking process invades your mind, it can be corrected. Those who know Jesus Christ as Savior have the opportunity to recover from the defects created in the human mind by the Fall. The Bible tells us Christians have the mind of Christ (see 1 Cor. 2:16), and our thoughts can be renewed by the Holy Spirit and our cooperation with the Word of God. (See Rom. 12:1-2; 2 Tim. 3:16-17.)

I would like you to consider using the series of questions below to evaluate your thoughts. These suggestions may seem overwhelming at first, but they can be very effective in bringing your thoughts to a constructive pattern during a period of crisis:

1. What is the basis for this thought? Is it a fact or just a negative thought? For example, do you tend to say, "I've always had difficulty in my relationships with the opposite sex, so why should I expect anything different?" That's a negative thought, not a fact of life. Look at all of the information and give yourself the benefit of the doubt.

2. Is it a mistake to assume the cause of my crisis? It is often difficult to determine causes. Sometimes we just don't know why certain things happen or why a person responds the way he does. And perhaps we will never fully know the answers. Often we look for—and naturally discover—the worst possible cause because of insufficient information.

3. Am I too close to the situation to know what really happened? Often during a breakup and its aftermath, your emotional response short-circuits your thinking process, so you find it difficult to determine what actually occurred. You may think, "If only I had responded differently, he wouldn't have left me. He just got tired of my defects." In light of the emotional pressure, how can you really know what the other person was thinking?

4. Am I thinking in "all or nothing" terms? "All or nothing" thinking reflects the view that life is only black or white, and people are only good or bad. This type of thinking is very limiting. Others do not treat you either all good or all bad. Life is a mixture of good and bad, and you will overlook the good in someone if you classify him as all bad for rejecting you.

5. *Do I use "ultimatum words" in my thinking?* You may say, "I *must* be accommodating and happy, or I won't attract another partner." This is an unfair and unrealistic ultimatum that reflects negative thinking. Ultimatum words like these must be countered with realistic answers.

Notice the following example. The negative thoughts belong to a young woman whose boyfriend left her for another woman. The young woman was attending college, where numerous other men were available. She countered her negative thoughts with realistic responses. (To chart a response to your own negative thoughts, see pages 159-160 of chapter 10.)

6. *Am I taking examples out of context?* A woman overheard two fellow employees talking about her. She thought she heard one of them say she was so rigid and dominant that she had trouble holding a man. Fortunately, she checked out the conversation with one of them and discovered they were describing her high standards and competence, which threatened a number of men! The words were spoken in a positive context, but because of her tendency to think the worst, she was tempted to distort the message.

7. *What is the source of my information?* Are your sources accurate, reliable, and trustworthy? Did you hear the information firsthand or secondhand? Did you hear the facts correctly? Did you ask others to repeat what they said so you can verify the content?

8. *What is the probability that what I fear will actually occur?* Your situation may be so rare or so correctable that there is little chance of your fear coming true. For example, a man feared that the woman he had been dating steadily for several weeks would think he didn't care about her since he hadn't seen her for a number of days. He was afraid she wouldn't want to see him again. But after thinking about it, he concluded they had been apart for several days before and she hadn't been upset. The probability of his fear coming true was very remote.

9. *Am I overlooking my strengths and capabilities?* A person

Negative thoughts	Answers
He shouldn't have left me for another woman.	I don't like it, but he should have left because he did. For all the reasons I don't know of, he should have left. I don't have to like it, just accept it.
I need him.	I want him back, but I don't need him. I need food, water, and shelter to survive. I don't need a man to survive. Thinking in terms of "needs" makes me vulnerable.
This always happens to me, and it will never change.	Just because it happened in one case doesn't mean it has happened or will happen in every case.
This is terrible, awful, horrible.	These are labels I add to the facts. The labels don't change anything, and they make me feel worse.
I must have someone to love me.	It's nice to love and be loved, but making it a condition to happiness is a way of putting myself down.
I'm too ugly and too fat to find anyone else.	"Too" is a relative concept, not some absolute standard. Thinking like this is self-defeating and stops me from trying.
I can't stand being alone.	I can stand difficulties—as I have in the past. I just don't like them.
I made a fool out of myself.	There's no such thing as a fool. Foolishness is only an abstraction, not something that exists. This mislabeling doesn't do me any good and makes me feel bad.
He made me depressed.	No one can make me feel depressed. I make myself depressed by the way I'm thinking.[3]

who is fearful about a new relationship tends to overlook his own positive qualities. He is overly critical of himself and focuses on his supposed defects instead of identifying his strengths. He wouldn't be as hard on his new love interest as he is on himself! He must balance his negative thinking with memories of the positive and constructive interactions he has enjoyed in past relationships.

10. *What do I actually want in this relationship?* For years I have asked counselees these questions to help them think through their goals in a relationship: "What do you want for your life? What do you want out of this relationship? How do you want to respond in this new relationship? What do you want from this other person? Can you envision yourself responding in a positive, healthy manner?"

11. *How would I approach this situation if I were not fearful about it?* Would I tend to make it worse than it is? Would I be as immobilized by fear as I am now? Again, imagine how you would respond if you believed you had the capabilities for handling whatever would occur.

12. *What can I do to solve my fearful condition?* Consider your thoughts. How are they leading to a solution for your fear? Write down your own solution to this fear. When was the last time you tried a different response to your fear? What will you do differently in your thought life and in your responses to others at this time?

13. *What are the distortions in my own thinking?* Are you aware of them? Who can help you identify them and correct them?

You may be thinking, "That's a lot of work to answer those questions!" Yes, it is. But your thought life will either prompt you to go forward in life or keep you bound to the past. And being bound to the past is a form of death.

Many admit to a fear of death. Many are afraid of the process of dying. But there is a fear more unsettling than either of these. It's the fear of getting to the end of your life and realizing it's been wasted, that you've never fully lived.

Unfortunately, many Christians never fully experience life because they live in fear. When you live in fear, you experience a form of death before you die. Fear freezes your life in place, prohibiting movement or progress, like a motion picture stuck on one frame. Fear will cause you to limit or neutralize your creative response to life. Don't let fear suffocate you. Live life to the fullest . . . without fear!

SEVEN
The Fear of Failure

The fear of failing drives us to rounds of relentless activity where satisfaction is never achieved.

When we allow the fear of failure to dominate us, we are demanding a guaranteed outcome in a situation. But a guarantee takes away the opportunity to live by faith and trust God for the outcome.

"Do not be afraid. Stand firm and you will see the deliverance the Lord will bring you today." (Exod. 14:13)

Years ago there was a TV game show in which contestants could choose unseen prizes from behind one of five doors on stage. Behind some of the doors were silly or embarrassing prizes, like a bucket of Jell-O or a pool of slimy mud. But behind one of the doors was a brand new Chevrolet Camaro.

It was interesting to watch how different types of contestants made their choices. Bold contestants looked at all the doors, confidently made a selection, opened a chosen door, and accepted the consequences graciously—good prize or bad. They didn't hesitate, and they weren't intimidated by the possibility of making the wrong decision.

Wishy-washy contestants looked at one door and then another, started toward one, stopped, went toward another, hesitated, and then, just before time ran out, plunged through the nearest door. But often when the wishy-washy contestants found a worthless prize on the other side of a door, they were very upset. Sometimes you could hear them berating themselves for their bad decisions.

Then there were the paralyzed contestants. They were unable to make a choice. They were so immobilized by the fear of making a wrong decision that the allotted time expired and they lost all opportunity to choose. "I just can't make up my mind," they would say. "I can't choose." Wrong! They did choose! How? By *not* choosing, they chose to lose.

People often choose to lose by failing to make decisions. When we were children, our parents cautioned us with the words, "Be careful not to make the wrong decision." And some of us still live by that creed. We are paranoid about making the right decisions. Wrong decisions, we reason, bring ridicule, embarrassment, and numerous negative consequences. So instead of risking a wrong decision, we make no decision, and, like the paralyzed contestants on the game show, we get nothing.

I remember many times in junior high school when the teacher posed a question to the class and I hesitated to volunteer an answer. I thought I knew the answer, but I wouldn't raise my hand because of the nagging fear that I might be wrong. On many occasions, I kicked myself afterward. I knew the correct answer, but I was afraid of making the wrong decision. Does that sound familiar? Too many people are devastated when their answer doesn't match the question, so they refuse to give an answer.

The fear of making a wrong decision reflects a lack of trust and self-confidence. This fear breeds additional fears and leads to vacillation and procrastination in many areas. The fear of a wrong decision is just one example of a common intimidating restraint—the fear of failure.

Nobody wants to fail

Failure—the very word ignites an uncomfortable feeling within most of us. We don't want to think about failure, much less experience it. The fear of failing drives some people to rounds of relentless activity where satisfaction is never achieved. The fear of failing inhibits many from stepping out and making progress. They live their lives mired in dissatisfaction, but they are unwilling to leave the safe confines of their stagnation because they are afraid they will only sink deeper into failure.

I've been afraid of failing; haven't you? Do you remember the teacher coming up to you and saying, "I'm sorry, you failed the exam." Can you recall the sinking feeling in the pit of your stomach when you saw the large, dark *F* on your report card? I can. Your entire world turned dark, especially when someone faced you with a smile and asked, "How did *your* grades turn out?"

What about the political candidate who invests enormous sums of money and hundreds of hours in a campaign—and loses? Failure! What about the creative time and thought that goes into the proposal you present to one of your clients—and they choose a competitor? Failure! What about the vast amounts of time, money, and emotion invested in courting someone you love—only to hear a firm no to your proposal of marriage? Failure!

Nobody enjoys failing. We all want to succeed and achieve. When we fail, we see ourselves as unsuccessful, perhaps even deficient or not good enough. There must be something wrong with us; that's why we failed!

Victimized by fear

When someone struggles with failure or the fear of failure long enough, he frequently ends up feeling like a victim. We hear stories about victims in the news every day—victims of robberies, assaults, unfair judgments, and other crimes or circumstances. At one time or another, all of us become victims of some event that is outside of our control. A victim is plagued by the sense of helplessness that seeps into his thinking processes.

There is a much more common type of victimization, however. It occurs with those who set themselves up to lose in the everyday activities of life. Those who fear failure, who tolerate the intolerable, who cooperate with those who take advantage of them or dominate them, who set themselves up to fail, or who blow issues out of proportion become emotional victims of their own creation.

There are various types of emotional victims. Some are exaggerators—people who may be real victims in some way, but who magnify the seriousness of the issue. Enlarging a problem through exaggeration enlarges your fear, especially the fear of failure. A counselee who recently had been divorced told me, "I failed in that marriage, and I doubt anybody else would want me. Who wants a failure? And if someone *did* want me, I don't think I could handle the new relationship. One failure is enough; I don't want another one."

Another type of emotional victim is the person who provokes victimization by others. This person sets himself up to be a victim. He acts in such a way as to elicit rejection. He lacks insight and perception in building relationships with others. Thus he often gets "burned" by others. He is afraid of failing and being taken advantage of, but it happens to him again and again. "Why me?" is a common response of this individual. "I don't want to fail. That's the last thing I want. I'm to the place where I'm almost afraid to try, and yet I know I will. But I don't want the same old problems to happen again."[1]

Isn't it interesting that some victims have a need to suffer, to fail, to be put down, or to be hurt? I met such a victim recently. John harbored a great amount of aggression, but he felt pressured to control his urge to strike out and hurt others. Yet his aggression needed an outlet, so he turned it against himself. He repeatedly set himself up to be a victim. He often blamed himself or got angry with himself for the bad things happening around him, which only increased his feelings and fear of failure.

Even though the fear of failure is often a central fear, there is an additional, underlying fear for emotional victims. It's the fear of being who they are. We live in a society that pressures us to conform. It takes courage to think and live differently than our culture's value system dictates. And if a person is afraid of what others think of him, he tends to hold back from being himself. Those who hold back end up being defensive, and the fear of failure is intensified.

The fear of failure, like other fears, comes from emotional reasoning, not factual reasoning. The helpless feelings that fear creates are spawned by incorrect thinking. The helpless feelings that characterize emotional victims come from the same faulty pattern of thinking. A life-changing principle to follow is: *If you don't think like a victim, you won't feel like a victim. If you don't think fearful thoughts, you won't be so fearful*. (See chapter 10 for practical steps to overcome fearful thoughts.)

Failure and the sexes

The fear of failure is a major stress point for men. Men have a great need to achieve and to feel they are in control. The fact that everyone makes mistakes is of little comfort to men in their moments of failure. Their competitive tendencies drive them to succeed for fear they will be dominated by others. Often their identities are so closely tied into their work that failing at work is tantamount to failing as a person.

The fear of failure at developing intimacy with a woman is prevalent among men in our society. Often I hear men in counseling say, "I can't open up to my wife and share how I really feel; I can't share who I am. Even if I tried, I'm afraid of her response. It's better to stay quiet."

For a man, even admitting his fear can be traumatic since it implies he is vulnerable and out of control. Emotional control is a high value in our culture's concept of masculinity. Since men don't like to acknowledge their fears, whenever they do seek counseling their problems are often more intense than a woman's.

Many men translate their fear response into anger. Admitting fear draws people close, and intimacy may be too threatening. But anger helps create a distance between a man and the people he fears. Anger is a mask he hopes will intimidate others and fool them into thinking he is in control. Anger is the camouflage many men use to hide their fears.[2]

The fear of failure pressures men to create a reservoir of excuses to avoid failure and remain in control. Have you heard (or used) any of the excuses described below?

● John avoided failure by putting things off. He would delay and stall on his tasks so he could say, "I had too little time, and that kept me from doing a better job."

● Sam tended to constantly overschedule himself. He would

say, "I just have too much to do. No one could possibly keep up with everything that's been dumped on me."

- Jim made everything he did extremely difficult. He always looked for the hardest way to complete a task. It was a great excuse to hide his fear of failure. After all, who could succeed with so many difficult tasks?

- Frank was a competent thirty-year-old man with a good work record, but his superiors were mystified over his refusal to complete forms and procedures for promotion. Frank was afraid of getting turned down for a new position, so he always found an excuse not to apply. He would rather stay in the safety of his present position.

I've heard many men (and women too) finally admit that it is less painful not to try than to try and fail!

Women also have a fear of failure, but much of it has been linked with the female's cultural legacy of nonassertiveness and passivity. Georgia Watkin-Lanoil, author of *The Female Stress Syndrome*, feels a woman's fear of failure is the result of years of being shamed or teased by men whenever she attempted a public performance of athletic, mechanical, or combative skill. It is fairly common, however, for a woman to feel both the need to achieve and the fear of failure at the same time. But fear tends to prevail and immobilize a woman because of her excessive concern over the opinions of others. And as this concern is often at its peak when she's with men, a woman collects her own array of excuses for failure to use when needed.[3]

From perfection to procrastination

The fear of failure is alive and well in those whom you would never suspect. A perfectionist is such a person. The perfectionist has a self-critic dwelling within him. He strives to do the impossible, places unrealistic demands on himself, and, when he is unable to meet those demands, feels overwhelmed. The perfectionist expects more of himself than he can attain.

A number of perfectionists were asked how they would define the word *perfectionism*. Notice their responses:

● "Doing something so well that nothing could make it better."
● "Doing nothing wrong; making no errors."
● "The need to have everything and everyone in just the right order."
● "The unreasonable desire to be perfect in every way."
● "Pushing yourself to reach an impossible goal."

No wonder perfectionists live with inner tension![4]

Perfectionism is driven by a familiar underlying force—the fear of failure. This fear causes perfectionists to live in a highly cautious, guarded manner. When a perfectionist is disappointed by his performance on a task, he doesn't think he has failed just on that task. He thinks he has failed as a person. Many perfectionists operate on the following formula:

1. What I produce is a reflection of how much ability I have.
2. My level of ability determines my worth as a person.
3. What I'm able to attain reflects my worth as a person.
4. Failure means I'm not worth much.

And so the fear of failure becomes a motivating force in the perfectionist's life.

To avoid failure, most perfectionists protect themselves by living in such a way that makes them appear anything but perfect: They procrastinate. As one man said, "If my best shot isn't going to make it, I'm not even going to try until I'm assured of success. I can't face being a failure, and I don't want the whole world to know."

Procrastination comes from two Latin words, *pro* meaning "forward" and *cras* meaning "the morrow." Literally, to procrastinate means to put something forward until the morrow—or, as we often quip, "Don't do today what you can put off till tomorrow." One author described procrastination as "the burglar of time, a thief which robs today of freedom and fills tomorrow with frustration."[5] But the perfectionist doesn't see procrastination this way, because his procrastination is serving a purpose. The perfectionist's motto is, "Do it later when you have a better chance to succeed."

Procrastination is a comfort to some people because it allows them to believe their ability is greater than their performance might be. After all, by procrastinating, you never really have to find out! Who wants to discover he *can't* do it when it's so much less painful to put it off and think he *can* do it? Meanwhile, he has a built-in excuse for his failure: "If I went ahead and tackled this project, it would be a breeze. But I just have so many other things taking up my time." The driving fear of failure is so strong that many perfectionists are willing to accept the consequences of procrastination. Admitting to laziness or disorganization is less painful than admitting to inadequacy.

A perfectionist is the type of person who will paint himself into a corner. He limits himself by erroneously believing there is only one correct solution to a problem, and he must find it. This is where procrastination enters in. Perfectionists are reluctant to act or commit to anything until they've discovered the correct solution. Some perfectionists make extensive lists of pros and cons, evaluate them, and then make more lists. But no matter how many factors are considered, final action—and the dreaded failure—are perpetually delayed.

The fear of failure paralyzes the perfectionist in his quest for adequacy. But for all believers—including perfectionists and those with occasional perfectionistic tendencies—adequacy always has been a free gift. God has declared us to be adequate because of what He has done for us through Jesus Christ. Any lack in our lives has been compensated for by God's free gift.

Yes, believers are called to be perfect. But it is a call to continually grow and mature, not to rid ourselves of mistakes or errors. Each of us can confidently express himself out of a sense of adequacy instead of striving for perfection.

We may as well accept it: You and I will never be perfect. If we are perfectionists, we will always be imperfect perfectionists. Why? Because the perfect world God created was marred by the fall of man, and we can never regain through our own efforts what was lost. Even knowing that, perfectionistic Christians continue to live as though they could perform perfectly. But it's impossible. Because of the Fall, we lost natural and ecological perfection, physical perfection, mental perfection, emotional perfection, relational perfection, and spiritual perfection. We've lost a lot! And no matter how much we strive through our own efforts, we can't earn what has already been lost.[6]

Remember that a perfectionistic person is a driven person, one who, upon making an outstanding accomplishment, cannot enjoy the results. He is like a pole vaulter in a major track meet. Every time the bar is raised, he clears it successfully. Gradually, his competitors are eliminated, and he wins the event. But does he rest and savor his victory? No. He asks the officials to raise the bar three inches higher. He tries and tries and tries to clear the bar, but fails each time. He feels terrible; he has failed. He cannot experience the joy of winning first place. He must do better. Unfortunately, many people are like this dissatisfied pole vaulter.

If you are a Christian perfectionist, part of your struggle is the cry of desperation that rises within you: "What if I fail? What if I'm not perfect?" Relax! I have an answer for you:

● You have failed in the past.
● You are failing now in some way.
● You will fail in the future.
● You weren't perfect in the past.
● You aren't perfect now.
● You won't be perfect in the future.

I like what David Seamands says about the issue of Christians and failure:

> To ask the question, "What if I fail?" is once again to attach strings to God's unconditional love and to change the nature of grace as undeserved and unearned favor. If your failure could stop grace, there would never be any such thing as grace. For the ground of grace is the Cross of Christ, and on the cross we were all judged as total fail-

ures. It was not a question of an occasional failure here and there. As far as our ability to bridge the moral canyon and win the approval of a Holy God, we are all total failures. In the Cross we were all examined and we all flunked completely![7]

You see, in spite of being a failure and not being perfect, you and I are loved and accepted by God. Seamands adds:

> God's love for us is unconditional; it is not a love drawn from God by something good in us. It flows out of God because of His nature. God's love is an action toward us, not a reaction to us. His love depends not on what we are but on what He is. He loves because He is love. We can refuse the love of God, but we cannot stop Him from loving us. We can reject it and thus stop its inflow into us, but we can do nothing to stop its outflow from Him. Grace is the unconditional love of God in Christ freely given to the sinful, the undeserving, and the imperfect.[8]

Failure will always be with us in this life. It's all right; it's normal. It's part of being human. When you fail, allow yourself to feel disappointment, but not disapproval. When you release your grip on perfectionism, the fear of failure will release its grip on you.[9]

Don't give up before trying

We all encounter tasks or problems in life that appear impossible. And when we face these mountains of impossibility, we are tempted to give up even before we try to scale them because we are convinced we will fail. But we quit before considering God's perspective of our situation. We're afraid we can't do anything and that God can't do anything, and so we do nothing.

I have found a scriptural example from the life of Moses and the Israelites that I think applies to our fear of failure. The following event took place shortly after Moses led the nation of Israel out of Egypt: "The Egyptians—all Pharaoh's horses and chariots, horsemen and troops—pursued the Israelites and overtook them as they camped by the sea near Pi Hahiroth, opposite Baal Zephon. As Pharaoh approached, the Israelites looked up, and there were the Egyptians, marching after them. They were terrified and cried out to the Lord" (Exod. 14:9-10).

The Israelites faced a seemingly impossible situation, and they were afraid. Their fear prompted them to complain to Moses, angrily blaming him for the apparent failure to which they had already conceded. They even said they would rather serve the Egyptians than die in the wilderness.

But listen to what Moses said to the people: "Do not be afraid. Stand firm and you will see the deliverance the Lord will bring you today. The Egyptians you see today you will never see again. The Lord will fight for you; you need only to be still" (Exod. 14:13-14). Then the Lord gave Moses directions for parting the sea, saying, "Tell the Israelites to move on" (Exod. 14:15).

Notice the steps of direction given in this passage:

1. *"Do not be afraid."* Lloyd Ogilvie suggests:

> Fear is usually the first reaction to our impossibility. Don't be afraid of fear. It reminds us we are alive, human. Like pain, it's a megaphone shout for God—a prelude to faith. The same channel of our emotions through which fear flows can be the riverbed for trust and loving obedience. Fear is only a hairbreadth away from faith. When we surrender our fear, telling God how we feel, we allow faith to force out fear. Tell God, "I'm afraid. I don't understand what you are doing with me! But I know there is something greater than this fear I feel. I know that you are in control and will allow nothing which will not bring me into deeper communion with you. What you give or take away is done that I might know you better." That's courageous praying in an impossibility. [10]

2. *"Stand firm."* Stand your ground. Don't give in to your fear and run away. Face your fear, allow yourself time to calm down, and then see the fear from God's perspective.

3. *"Be still."* Sometimes we are so frantic and noisy with our fear that we override God's direction, God's peace, and God's presence in our lives. We can be helped by quietly listening for His voice to guide us.

4. *"Move on."* This is what God said. When confronted with something we fear, we can run from it and give it control over us. Or we can face it, move toward it, and eventually neutralize it. When we fail to move on, we procrastinate, and procrastination is not God's plan for us. Procrastination is fear that has forgotten the promises of God. It is our effort to make life stand still for a while when God has clearly instructed us to keep moving.

Another scriptural example is the story of the twelve spies Moses sent to spy out the Promised Land. (See Numbers 13:1-33.) The spies returned from their mission with two very different reports. Ten of the spies feared failure and voted to procrastinate because their enemies in the land were large and numerous. The ten complained, "We seemed like grasshoppers in our own eyes, and we looked the same to them" (Num. 13:33). The way you view yourself dictates the way you will act. If you see yourself as inadequate, you will be inadequate. Your fear becomes a self-fulfilling prophecy.

But Caleb and Joshua were ready to trust God and move on despite the odds. Caleb said, "We should go up and take possession of the land, for we can certainly do it" (Num. 13:30). Going forward shrinks fears; procrastinating only enlarges them.[11]

Make the most from your mistakes

Most of us think of a failure as a negative experience. But we all fail at times, and we all make occasional mistakes. We must learn to use our failures to our advantage and grow from them.

Consider these suggestions for making the most from your mistakes:

1. *One mistake or failure does not mean everything is ruined.* Look for the success and achievement in every situation in which you experience a failure. If you cannot find the positives among the negatives, you're caught up in the fallacy of perfectionistic thinking. Whenever you feel you have failed, write down the areas in which you didn't fail. This exercise will help you keep the situation in proper balance.

2. *Mistakes provide us with excellent learning opportunities.* Most of us don't learn or grow unless we make mistakes. I've even heard some people refer to their mistakes as "corrective ventures" and "growth experiences." You can't outrun your mistakes, so turn around, face them, and learn from them.

3. *Failures help us adjust our behavior so we can get the results we want.* Failures can actually make things better. For example, in 1980 I took up racquetball. During the first four months, I made every mistake in the book and then some! I "failed" every game; I never won. But I kept working to improve my poor shots and one day my failures paid off—I actually won a game. I still lose some games, but my failures help me focus on what I must do differently in the next game *not* to lose.

4. *Trial and error keeps you from getting paralyzed.* Have you ever sat with your legs crossed for a long period of time, then tried to stand and discovered that one leg was asleep? For a few seconds you were paralyzed, stuck, immobilized.

When you don't try anything for fear of failure, you are paralyzed. When you restrict your life so you don't make mistakes, you end up making the greatest mistake of all. You deny yourself the opportunity to develop all the capabilities God has given to you. He wants you to risk, to reach out. He would rather have you try and occasionally fail than to sit paralyzed by fear. And He is with you each step of the way.

5. *You can learn to live with imperfection.* I'd like you to write down on a separate sheet of paper a list of reasons that you're afraid of failure. I've heard many of them. Here are a few:

- "Other people will laugh at me."
- "Other people won't think much of me and will probably even get mad at me."
- "Other people won't like me."
- "If I make one mistake, I'll probably continue to make others."
- "God doesn't love me as much when I fail."
- "The feeling of failure is more than I can take. I just can't handle it."
- "When I fail, I confirm what my parents said about me. And I'm not going to do anything to prove them right!"

Every one of these reasons—including the ones on your list—can be challenged. You won't die or develop worms in your stomach when you make a mistake. Face it: You are imperfect, and you can learn to handle being imperfect. [12]

6. *The fear of failure will lift when you begin to view your life from God's perspective.* This is perhaps the most important suggestion of all. When you face a potential failure, ask God for His strength and wisdom to handle either the success or the attempt. Ask Him how you can use the failure for His glory and your growth.

Sometimes we set ourselves up for failure by trying to accomplish our goals alone. When Abraham was called by God to leave his homeland to become the father of a great nation, the possibilities for failure were enormous—at least from Abraham's perspective. He knew his strength and wisdom were insufficient for the task. He had doubts and fears about the outcome. But God simply asked Abraham to trust Him for the completion of the task. Sure, Abraham made some mistakes along the way, but he is chiefly remembered for the successes that his faith in God produced.

When we allow the fear of failure to dominate us, we are demanding a guaranteed outcome in the situation. But a guaranteed outcome takes away the opportunity to live by faith and trust God for the outcome. Faith is what makes life fulfilling. That's how change occurs. That's how great ministries develop.

Decisions, decisions, decisions

At the beginning of the chapter, we discussed the fear of making a wrong decision, as illustrated by the paralyzed, wishy-washy game show contestants. If you were sitting in my counseling office and expressed your concern over making the wrong decision, I would probably respond by asking, "What's a wrong decision? What would make your decision wrong?" Interesting questions. I've asked them many times, and I've heard many responses. For example:

- "It was a bad decision because things didn't turn out the way I wanted."
- "The result of my decision wasn't what I was hoping for."
- "The decision is wrong when the results are upsetting or hurtful."
- "I'm not sure I can handle the results of a wrong decision."

All of these answers suggest that a decision is wrong based upon the kind of result it produces. Many fear wrong decisions because they fear the wrong results of their decisions.

But we place too much emphasis upon the results of our decisions and fail to realize the value of the process. Often what we call a wrong decision can be a right decision regardless of the results. I've made some decisions that produced results different from the ones I wanted. I've wasted time berating myself for my bad decision and wondering, What would have happened if . . . ?

Over the years, I've learned to ask myself questions that help me reinterpret my wrong decisions as decisions that enabled me to learn something I hadn't anticipated learning. Here are the questions I use:

- What was the actual outcome of the decision?
- Why was the outcome so bad? (Sometimes it can be classified as unpleasant and undesirable instead of bad.)
- What did I learn apart from the unexpected results?
- How am I a different person today because the results were different than I anticipated?
- What will I do differently the next time I face this decision?

It would be nice if every decision you made produced the results you wanted. But wrong decisions and their results are not the end of the world. Answering these questions can help you discover the good in a bad decision. This process may also help you realize that God has different plans in mind for you.

Recently, a client expressed her hesitation in making a decision. She asked, "What if it doesn't work out as planned?" Then she told me the outcome she desired from the decision.

We explored the possibility of her realizing 50 percent of the desired outcome. "Would it still be a correct decision at 50 percent return?" I asked. She said it would. We worked it down to 25 percent and then 10 percent, and at each step she agreed that the decision would still be right. Then I said, "Perhaps the end result isn't so important after all. Could it be that the right decision is just to make a decision and learn through the process after the decision is made?"

She thought for a moment, then smiled and said, "I think I see what you're driving at." As she learned to trust herself and evaluate her decisions in a different way, her confidence increased and her fears diminished.

Those who survive difficult situations and gain the most from life are those who are flexible and learn to adapt and change.[13] Stewart Emery, who wrote *Actualizations*, gives a helpful illustration of this process. During a flight to Hawaii, Emery rode on the plane's flight deck. One of the instruments that caught his attention was the inertial guidance system. The pilot explained that the function of the instrument was to guide the giant plane to within 1,000 yards of the runway within five minutes of the estimated arrival time. The system continually and automatically corrected the plane's course to achieve its programmed goal. Even though the plane was off course 90 percent of the time, the destination was reached by the process of making repeated course corrections.

We need to listen to and learn from our internal guidance systems and make the necessary course corrections in our lives. When we are not enjoying the desired outcome from our decisions, we either need to make a course change or learn to appreciate what we gain from the decision evaluation process.[14]

For more than twenty years I have taught graduate courses at Talbot Theological Seminary in La Mirada, California. From time to time, students have come to my office to share their decision to leave the seminary. Some were confused because they thought their decision to attend in the first place was wrong or that leaving was a sign of failure. But other departing students had a positive outlook on the process, saying, "My decision to attend the seminary was not a wrong decision. The year I spent here was excellent. It showed me that pastoral ministry is not my calling. I'm going in another direction now, and leaving the seminary is just a course correction."

How can you confront your fear of making decisions? What is the decision you're most fearful of making at this time? Let's take the questions I shared earlier and reword them for you to use. Apply these questions to the decision you're struggling with at this time:

- What is the actual outcome I want from the decision?
- What are some alternative outcomes that may result from my decision?
- Where is my fear and lack of trust coming from?
- What can I learn from the decision-making process?
- This is what I will do to make the process more important than the outcome:

Remember: By not deciding, you are deciding to let something or someone else decide for you. And that's a form of bondage! Why not discuss your decisions with Jesus Christ, search His Word for guidance, ask for His wisdom, and then decide. Once you decide, take action. Become a Caleb!

EIGHT
The Fear of Success

The fear of success is one of the great mysteries of life.

The fear of success is a thief that robs us of the enjoyments of life.

Jesus Christ can enable you to handle your success.

See your ability and strength as a gift from God. He can help you override your fear.

"For God did not give us a spirit of timidity." (2 Tim. 1:7)

It's called sabotage. Its mission is to hinder, obstruct, waste, or destroy in order to prevent success. It is performed by an opponent or an enemy. It is carried out subtly and covertly.

Sabotage happens in war when trained saboteurs sneak behind enemy lines to blow up bridges, interrupt supply lines, or disrupt battle plans. It happens in politics when one candidate stoops to rumor-starting, mudslinging, or character assassination in order to discredit his opponent. It happens in sports when one racing team secretly tampers with the engine of a rival team's car in order to gain an advantage on the track.

But perhaps the most sinister and personally destructive act of sabotage is that which is performed by an individual on himself. Self-sabotage? Yes. Incredible, but true. There are many people who become their own enemy, who subtly—often subconsciously—behave so as to hinder, obstruct, waste, or destroy their opportunities in order to prevent their own success. And the root of this destructive behavior is a confusing and perplexing fear: the fear of success.

"Afraid of success? Where did you get a wild idea like that? I love success!" That was the response I received from a forty-five-year-old company vice-president when I suggested he may be suffering from a fear of success. His response reflects the attitude of many people who cannot conceive of being afraid of success.

But this fear is common, even highly prevalent today. It is severe in some people and minimal in others. The fear of success is like a thief that robs us of success or of the enjoyment of success.

I see the fear of success in the college student who works hard during the semester, then for some unexplained reason chooses not to study for the final exam. I see it in the actress who fails to show up for her final audition, even though she knows her lines perfectly and has succeeded in preliminary auditions. I see it in the executive who makes an unexplainable mistake in an area of his expertise, and his mistake keeps him from the presidency of the company he has served for twenty-three years.

If you were to ask these three, "What happened? Why did you sabotage your success?" they might give you a reasonable excuse, but they probably wouldn't know the real answer. Here's what some have said about their problems with success:

- "When I'm successful, I wonder if I'll be able to sustain my level of work. If I let down at all, I'll be seen as a huge failure."
- "I felt much better when I was just a salesman. When they made me the manager, I wasn't sure I could do what they wanted. And I didn't have the camaraderie with the other salespeople I had before."
- "All my life I've fought being successful. Why? I'll tell you. When something good happens to me, I know I'll have to pay for it in some way."
- "I have the feeling that if I'm successful, something might come along and spoil it. And then I will feel worse than if I hadn't succeeded."

For many, the only results of success are feelings of anxiety, guilt, inadequacy, and frustration.

Fear has a price tag

The fear of success can sabotage even the most successful individuals. Mary Pickford was one of the first great female movie stars and remains a legend in the world of entertainment. She enjoyed enormous social and economic power and was admired by millions.

But Mary Pickford admitted she was obsessed by the fear of success. For her, the pursuit of success was like climbing to the top of a flagpole. The climb was tough, and she had to fight others who wanted to beat her to the top. Because she attained such lofty success, Pickford felt she lost all sense of relationship with those below her. She said, "Perspective becomes distorted; a widening gulf develops. It's cold atop the flagpole. Winds howl. To make matters worse, the pole is greased. If I slip, the descent is all the way to the bottom. People who envy me hurl mud and rocks in an attempt to dislodge me."[1]

The fear of success has led to some very tragic consequences for some. Even successful celebrities can be driven by fear into loneliness and isolation. Mary Pickford eventually became a recluse in her own estate. The fear of success can keep any of us from enjoying whatever success we have achieved.

Giving in to the fear of success not only exacts a toll on us, but on people around us. I remember a football coach who saw some untapped potential in a new player. The young man possessed tremendous athletic ability and two strong, agile legs. The coach worked diligently to teach the boy one skill: kicking the extra points after touchdowns. Day after day on the practice field, the coach helped the kicker develop his skill and timing and encouraged him in his progress. Soon the boy could kick the football through the goalposts easily and accurately.

In the first game, the other team held a 6-0 lead late in the game. But with only seconds to play, the kicker's team scored a touchdown, tying the score, and lined up near the goal line for the extra point. Based on the kicker's skill in practice, the extra point was almost automatic and the victory assured. The ball was snapped, the linemen held their blocks, and the holder placed the ball perfectly for the kick.

But for some strange reason, instead of kicking the ball, the kicker dived on it to keep it from the other team. In his pressure-filled moment of fear, the competent kicker chose to play it safe rather than to risk success. His fear affected his entire team and their football season.

This story reminds me of the parable of the talents in Matthew 25:14-30. Read the parable and consider how the fear of success may have affected the behavior of those to whom the talents were given.

Telltale signs of fear

How can you tell when the fear of success is subtly sabotaging your activities? What are some of the common telltale signs that may help you identify and deal with your fear or others' fears?

Remember, very few people ever reveal they are afraid of success. And even fewer people understand the reasons behind their fear or its manifestations. The fear of success is one of the great mysteries of our society. And those who are involved with a fearful person may inadvertently reinforce the fear by the way they respond.

Procrastinating. It's amazing that procrastination emerges so often as the means by which many cope with their fears. People procrastinate when they fear failure, and they also procrastinate when they fear success. A worker may slow down on a project that is going along quite well. A PTA officer may arrive late for—or avoid altogether—a ceremony honoring her for her tire-less work. Why? Because delaying the event of success or recognition keeps them a safe distance away from their fear of success or recognition. They wish they could break free and move ahead. In fact, they are often critical of themselves for their procrastination. But a spirit of fear seems to dominate them.

Avoiding competition. Those who fear success tend not to be competitive. They're not afraid of losing; they're afraid of winning. Instead of moving ahead, competing, and winning, they hold back so others won't be able to see their ambition. Whenever they are pitted competitively against another, they take themselves out of the running. Why? For some reason, they feel it is wrong to be competitive. They live with a fear of defeating others because it may violate their moral code.

Avoiding work. Jim came to me for counseling for several weeks. One day, he finally told me why he thought he was crippling his own efforts in his job: "Norm, I'm afraid of becoming a workaholic. Some of the people in my office are addicted to their work, and I don't want to become like them. I know I'm good at what I do, but I don't want to be tied down to that job day and night. If I begin to climb the ladder of success, I'm afraid I'll catch the disease. I've seen it happen. I like my free time, and I'm going to hold onto it."

Jim's comments are interesting but not unusual. Many people don't put out their best efforts on the job because, like Jim, they are afraid their jobs will control them.

Have these fears ever entered your mind? If so, think for a minute: Who said you are doomed to become a workaholic? What an opportunity you have to demonstrate to workaholics that it's possible to work hard and still leave the office on time and enjoy your weekends! The motto is "Don't work longer, work smarter." Avoiding work is one way to keep the pressure to succeed from swallowing you up, but a better way is to set your goals, work steadily, and say "no" firmly when necessary.

Perhaps there is another underlying fear that causes some people to avoid work. I wonder if they are afraid they'll enjoy success so much that they really will become addicted to it? That's a possibility—except when your self-esteem, identity, and priorities are rooted in Jesus Christ. If He is in charge of your life, your work and success will stay in balance.

Avoiding commitments. The fear of success also drives people to avoid making commitments. By avoiding commitment, you also avoid the competition and work in which you may succeed.

Why people fear success

There are several reasons behind these telltale signs that explain why some people sabotage their own success. Let's discuss some of the most prominent:

Success saboteurs resist cultural risks. Even in this era of sexual equality, cultural sex role barriers still exist which cause some people to avoid success. Many women are influenced by beliefs that stand against their personal success. Years ago, a woman's role was to assist a man to be successful but not to be successful in her own right. Many women today are still uncomfortable with personal success and anticipate social rejection. Some women choose to live with this inner tension—to be successful in their own right, but to fear the consequences of it. This pattern produces many of the telltale signs of fear that were described in the previous paragraphs.

Men are not free from cultural influences either. Men are generally expected to fulfill the roles of husband, father, adequate provider, and church and community leader. But many men are afraid they can't live up to these traditional expectations. Others tend to avoid success in these roles for fear of being trapped in them. They want greater freedom in life. As one forty-year-old man put it, "If I succeed in all these roles, I'll be expected to occupy them for the rest of my life. I don't want to get myself into that kind of a rut. So what if others think I'm a bit flaky! I have more freedom this way and it's worth the few hassles I get." I'm sure many men feel this way, but few are honest enough to admit it.

Success saboteurs don't feel they deserve success. Dolores was a well-groomed businesswoman who held a responsible position at her company. She told me, "In a way, I like what I do. And the sky's the limit for me in this company. They like me and encourage me, but I hesitate. I'm afraid to make that last push to be really successful."

"Could it be that you're struggling with being too successful?" I replied.

"I think so," Dolores admitted. "The success I do attain bothers me."

"Are you aware of the reason?" I asked. Silence. "Could it be that you feel you don't deserve to be successful?"

Again, silence. And then the tears began to come. "You know, I've always wanted to be successful, and many times I have been," Dolores confessed hesitantly. "But it's always the same. I get to the top, but I don't enjoy it. I don't feel I deserve to be there. It's as though I've hurt others, and I shouldn't be successful. Instead of enjoying my success, I feel like I should be doing penance for some sin I've committed. I don't understand these feelings!"

For some, the remorse they experience in their success is rightfully tied to past behaviors that were wrong. But for others, it's just a feeling. Either way, the feeling keeps them from success. When feelings like this persist, it is usually helpful to spend time with a trained counselor or minister who can help you sort through past events and messages that may be contributing to the present fear.[2]

If you are experiencing fear or guilt because you don't feel worthy of the success you achieve, complete the following exercise on a separate sheet of paper:

1. Who are the people in your life who have said, "You don't deserve success?" Write down their names and the reasons they have given.

2. Who are the people who believed in you and encouraged you to be successful? Write down their names and what they have said to you.

3. Why would you like to be successful? List your reasons.

4. How will you use your success for yourself? For the glory of God?

The next time you feel you don't deserve success, challenge the feeling. Tell yourself why you deserve success and why you're going to move ahead and enjoy the results of your efforts. Give this irrational fear to Jesus Christ. He has not given us a spirit of controlling fear. He has given us peace and freedom from guilt. If there is something in the past that we shouldn't have done, it is forgiven and blotted out by the work of Jesus Christ for us. Enjoy your freedom in Him.

Success saboteurs are afraid they will offend others with their success. Meg told me an interesting reason for her fear of success: "I guess I'm one of the fortunate ones because I've had a lot of good things happen to me in my life. I should be able to enjoy my successes, but every time something good happens, I'm afraid to share it with others. I don't want them to feel bad or to be offended.

"In college, when I earned an A, I couldn't tell my two best friends. We always studied together, but no matter how hard they worked they were lucky to pull Bs and Cs. But I'd usually cram the night before and come out with an A. I never felt very good about it. I guess I'm afraid that my good news is bad news to someone else."

Meg's not alone. Many of us are afraid of offending others. We're concerned about being a discouragement to our friends or to our spouses. One tough area of adjustment is where both the husband and wife work. She gets the promotions and raises, and eventually she ends up making more money than her husband. Some women struggle with their financial success for fear that it will threaten their husbands and weaken their marriages.

Perhaps some people may be bothered by your success. But isn't that more their problem than your problem? Most people delight in another's success without being hurt or bitter. Give others credit for being able to handle your success and rejoice with you. Those who cannot have to deal with their own problems. You cannot rescue them or allow their insecurity to affect your capability. You *can* encourage and affirm them.

Success saboteurs resist responsibility. Fred had seven jobs in ten years, and he procrastinated in each one of them. It was unfortunate, since he had ability and his employers had anticipated great things from him.

But Fred sabotaged any potentially successful activity that might place him in the limelight. He told me, "I don't want the responsibility. The bigger the job, the bigger the headaches. The more responsibility I assume, the more grief I suffer, and the more I can be hurt and badgered by others. That's not for me. Sure, the money would be nice, but less responsibility is more comfortable." And so Fred lived in a state of fear, believing he had to protect himself from other capable people.

How does this happen? You may have learned this pattern as a child. You may have had an angry, impatient parent who reacted negatively every time you shared an achievement or a dream. Or perhaps jealous classmates in school made life a bit unbearable when you achieved. Enough experiences like this can create a distorted thinking pattern. You soon learn to keep your dreams to yourself and not to try too hard to succeed.

Success saboteurs suffer from low self-esteem. There is one other reason for being afraid of success. Its potential lurks within every one of us. We call it low self-esteem, a low opinion of oneself. When you believe yourself to be unskilled, inadequate, and unable to obtain your goals or dreams, you don't bother to try. And when any type of success does fall your way, you don't enjoy it. You learn not to hope. That eases the pain and possibility of disappointment.[3]

Successfully dismissing your fear of success

I've been asked the question more than once: "How do I overcome my fear of success?" The obvious answer is to succeed. Here is a step-by-step process that will help you turn your fear into success—if you practice these steps consistently.

1. Identify the origin of your fear as clearly as possible.

2. Write down what you consider to be two valid reasons for your fear. (Every reason given in this chapter for not achieving success is, in fact, a myth.) Then list six reasons for not fearing success in this area. As you write, the basis for your behavior will be destroyed.

3. Describe thoroughly the successes you have already attained in this area. Most individuals allow themselves success up to a certain point and then back off. Go all the way with your list.

4. List specifically how you will be praying for this concern in your life.

5. Select two or three trusted individuals and share your

concern with them. Ask them to believe in you, encourage you, and pray for you.

6. Allow yourself to experience the success. After some time has elapsed, evaluate the benefits of being successful. They may surprise you.

7. Had you considered that the area in which you are struggling with success could be the realm in which God has endowed you with spiritual gifts? Could He be the author of your ability and strength? He is a giver, and we can count on His gifts to be successful!

Perhaps if you begin to see your ability and strength as a gift from God, you may be able to override your fear. If He has given you the ability in the first place, won't He give you the ability to handle the results? Ask Him to assist you in handling the pressures of your success. When you do, your success can be used for the glory of God. And that could change someone else's life too!

NINE

Worry—First Cousin to Fear

Worry is a pessimistic glance into the future.

Worry brings about our worst fears.

Worry is a war quietly raging within us.

"All the days of the desponding afflicted are made evil [by anxious thoughts and foreboding], but he who has a glad heart has a continual feast [regardless of circumstances]." (Prov. 15:15, AMP)

She sat in my office appearing to be self-assured and totally in control of her life. When I asked her why she had made an appointment to see me, she surprised me by saying, "It's the dreams I've been having for the last few months. Several times a week I dream I'm being choked. In each dream, there's a hand squeezing my throat so I almost can't breathe. I'm here to see if you can help me figure out what my dreams mean."

I replied, "The first thought that comes to mind is a question: Are you a worrier? Do you tend to worry about . . ."

Before I could finish, she interrupted me. "I could earn an achievement award for my worrying ability," she said cynically. "I'm so good at worrying, I could be a professional worrier. But what caused you to ask me about worry?" When I explained to her the definition of the word, she realized the message her dreams were conveying to her.

Worry comes from an Anglo-Saxon root meaning "to strangle" or "to choke." Worry is the uneasy, suffocating feeling we often experience in times of fear, trouble, or problems. When we worry, we look pessimistically into the future and think of the worst possible outcome to the situations of our lives. Worry is the unnecessary fretting and stewing that keeps our minds stirred up and our stomachs churning. Dr. W. C. Alvarez of Mayo Clinic says, "Eighty percent of the stomach disorders that come to us are not organic, but functional. . . . Most of our ills are caused by worry and fear."[1] Intense worry is about as useful to our thinking as lighted matches in a dynamite factory.

Worry is like a war that is quietly raging inside us. John Haggai describes the conflict this way:

> Worry divides the feelings, therefore the emotions lack stability. Worry divides the understanding, therefore convictions are shallow and changeable. Worry divides the faculty of perception, therefore observations are faulty and even false. Worry divides the faculty of judging, therefore attitudes and decisions are often unjust. These decisions lead to damage and grief. Worry divides the determinative faculty, therefore plans and purposes, if not "scrapped" altogether, are not filled with persistence.[2]

If fear and worry are first cousins, worry and anxiety have an even closer relationship. Worry and anxiety both refer to the inner turmoil we experience in fearful, stressful situations. The Greeks described anxiety as opposing forces at work to tear a man apart.

But not all anxiety is bad; it has a plus side. As Dr. Quentin Hyder suggests in *The Christian's Handbook of Psychiatry*, "A little [anxiety] in normal amounts can enhance performance. Athletes would be unable to perform successfully without it. Businessmen do better in their competitive world than they could do without its stimulus. It definitely strengthens concentration and spurs imagination, thereby producing more creative ideas. It stimulates interest and develops ambition. It protects from danger."[3] In its positive sense anxiety is a God-given instinct that alerts us to fearful situations and prepares us to respond.

The negative aspects of worry and anxiety must also be differentiated from positive concern in troublesome situations. Pastor Earl Lee illustrates the difference: "Worry is like racing an automobile engine while it is in neutral. The gas and noise and smog do not get us anywhere. But legitimate concern . . . is putting the car into low gear on your way to moving ahead. You tell yourself that you are going to use the power God has given you to do something about the situation which could cause you to fret."[4] Worry immobilizes you and does not lead to action. But concern moves you to overcome the problem.

Many Scripture verses describe the effects of fear, worry, and anxiety. And many other verses reveal that a worry-free life reaps many positive rewards. Notice the contrast in the verses below:

- "I heard, and my [whole inner self] trembled, my lips quivered at the sound. Rottenness enters into my bones and under me—down to my feet—I tremble" (Hab. 3:16, AMP).
- "Anxiety in a man's heart weighs it down" (Prov. 12:25, AMP).
- "A tranquil mind gives life to the flesh" (Prov. 14:30, RSV).
- "All the days of the desponding afflicted are made evil [by anxious thoughts and foreboding], but he who has a glad heart has a continual feast [regardless of circumstances]" (Prov. 15:15, AMP).
- "A happy heart is a good medicine and a cheerful mind works healing, but a broken spirit dries the bones" (Prov. 17:22, AMP).
- "A glad heart makes a cheerful countenance, but by sorrow of heart the spirit is broken" (Prov. 15:13, AMP).

What are you worried about?

What do people worry about? It would be safe to say *everything*. Dr. Samuel Kraines and Eloise Thetford suggest three categories into which most worries fall:

1. Disturbing situations for which one must find a *solution*—for example, how to obtain money for food, lodging, or medical expenses.
2. Disturbing situations over which one has *no control*—for example, a mother dying of cancer, a usually prompt

daughter who is five hours late, or a son in active combat.

3. Unimportant, insignificant, *minor problems of every-day life which warrant little attention*, let alone "worry." People "worry" about minor details of everyday life, concocting horrible possibilities and then "stewing" about them. The housewife "worries" that she cannot clean the house as she once did, does not iron the clothes well, and cannot prepare proper meals. The man "worries" that he is doing poorly at work, that he will be "fired," and that he "cannot pay his bills." The list goes on and on. The worry is not only a feeling tone of fearfulness but an overriding sense of futility, hopelessness, and dreaded possibilities.[5]

Worrying intensely about the possibility of some event happening not only does not prevent it from happening but can actually help to bring it about. A young seminary student is waiting to preach his first sermon. He sits thinking about what he is going to say. He begins to worry about forgetting words, stumbling over certain phrases, and not presenting himself in a confident manner. As he continues to worry, he actually sees himself making these mistakes. And then when he gets up to preach, he makes the very mistakes he worried about!

If you were to tell him that he shouldn't worry about his preaching, he would reply, "I was justified in worrying. After all, those problems that I worried about were real problems. They happened, didn't they? I should have been worried!" What he does not realize is that by his own worry he actually helped them occur. He was responsible for his own failure. He spent more time seeing himself fail than he did visualizing himself succeed or overcome his fears.

The principle here is that if you spend time seeing yourself as a failure, you will more than likely reproduce that example in your performance. You actually condition yourself for negative performances because of your negative thinking. The classic example is the person who worries about getting an ulcer and, in a few months, is rewarded for his efforts with an ulcer. People who continually worry about having an accident on the freeway are very accident-prone. They are more likely to have accidents than others because they constantly visualize the event.

However, if you spend the same amount of time and energy planning how to overcome your anticipated mistakes and visualizing your success as you do visualizing your failure, your performance will be far better. Proverbs 23:7 tells us that the way we think in our hearts determines what we do.

The final results of fear, worry, and anxiety are negative, self-defeating, and incapacitating. What do we accomplish by worrying? Are there any positive results? Make a list of the things you worry about, then describe specifically what the worry has accomplished or will accomplish. Does it solve the problem or does it create more problems?

When you worry about a problem, real or imaginary, it usually impedes you from being able to do something effective about the problem. Worry is a problem. But rejoice—there is a solution.

Scriptural resources for worry

Does worry have any place in the life of the Christian? Is it a sin to worry or to feel anxiety?

A person who experiences extreme states of anxiety may not be able to control them. He may feel he is at the mercy of his feelings because he cannot pin down exactly why he is so anxious. This person may have deep, hidden feelings or hurts that have lingered for years in the unconscious. In such a case, perhaps he needs to face a problem, discover the roots of his feelings, and replace them with the healing power and resources offered through Jesus Christ and Scripture.

Anxiety may stem from unconscious feelings. But worry is a conscious act of choosing an ineffective method of coping with life. Oswald Chambers has said that all our fret and worry is caused by calculating without God. Worry actually implies the absence of trust in God. And since Scripture specifically instructs us *not* to worry, this lack of trust in the Lord is certainly sin.

But freedom from worry *is* possible. The answer lies in tapping the resources of Scripture. Read each passage cited below before reading the paragraphs that follow it.

Worry doesn't work, so don't do it (Matthew 6:25-34). From this passage, we can discover several principles to help us overcome anxiety and worry. First, note that Jesus did *not* say, "Stop worrying when everything is going all right for you." He simply and directly said to stop worrying about your life. In a way, Jesus was saying we should learn to accept situations that cannot be altered at the present time. That doesn't mean we're to sit back and make no attempt to improve conditions around us. But we must face tough situations without worry and learn to live with them while we work toward improvement.

Second, Jesus said you cannot add any length of time to your life span by worrying. In reality, the reverse is true. The physical effects of worry can actually shorten your life span.

Third, the object of our worry may be part of the difficulty. It could be our sense of values is distorted and that what we worry about should not be the center of our attention. The material items that seem so important to us should be secondary to spiritual values.

Fourth, Christ also recommends we practice living a day at a time. You may be able to change some of the results of past behavior, but you cannot change the past, so don't worry about it. You cannot predict or completely prepare for the future, so don't inhibit its potential by worrying about it. Focus your energies on the opportunities of today!

Most of the future events people worry about don't happen anyway. Furthermore, the worrisome anticipation of certain inevitable events is usually more distressing than the actual experience. Anticipation is the magnifying glass of our emotions. And even if an event *is* as serious as we may anticipate, the Christian can look forward to God's supply of strength and stability at all times.

Focus on the solution, not the problem (Matthew 14:22-33). In this passage, we find the disciples in a boat as Jesus walked toward them on the water. When Peter began to walk toward Jesus on the water, he was fine until his attention was drawn away from Jesus to the storm. Then he became afraid and started to sink.

If Peter had kept his attention upon Christ (the source of his strength and the solution to his problem), he would have been all right. But when he focused upon the wind and the waves (the problem and the negative aspect of his circumstances), he became overwhelmed by the problem—even though he could have made it safely to Jesus!

Worry is like that. We focus so hard on the problem that we take our eyes off the solution and thus create more difficulties for ourselves. We can be sustained in the midst of any difficulty by focusing our attention on Jesus Christ and relying upon Him.

Give God your worry in advance (1 Peter 5:7). Peter must have learned from his experience of walking on the water because he later wrote: "Cast all your anxiety on him [God] because he cares for you." Cast means "to give up" or "to unload." The tense of the verb here literally refers to a direct, once-and-for-all committal to God of all anxiety or worry. We are to unload on God our tendency to worry so that when problems arise, we will not worry about them. We can cast our worry on God with confidence because He cares for us. He is not out to break us down, but to strengthen us and to help us stand firm. He knows our limits, and "a bruised reed he will not break, and a dimly burning wick he will not quench" (Isa. 42:3, RSV).

Center your thoughts on God, not on worry (Isaiah 26:3). Isaiah rejoiced to the Lord, "You will guard him and keep him in perfect and constant peace whose mind [both its inclination and its character] is stayed on You" (AMP). Whatever you choose to think about will either produce or dismiss feelings of anxiety and worry. Those who suffer from worry are choosing to center their minds on negative thoughts and to anticipate the worst. But if your mind or imagination is centered on God—what He has done and will do for you—and the promises of Scripture, peace of mind is inevitable. But you must choose to center your thoughts in this way. God has made the provision, but you must take the action. Freedom from worry and anxiety is available, but you must lay hold of it.

Replace fretting with trust (Psalm 37:1-40). Psalm 37:1 begins, "Do not fret," and those words are repeated later in the chapter. The dictionary defines "fret" as "to eat away, gnaw, gall, vex, worry, agitate, wear away."

Whenever I hear this word, I'm reminded of the scene I see each year when I hike along the Snake River in the Grand Teton National Park in Wyoming. Colonies of beavers live along the riverbanks, and often I see trees that are at various stages of being gnawed to the ground by them. Some trees have slight rings around their trunks where the beavers have just started to chew on them. Other trees have several inches of bark eaten away, and some have already fallen to the ground because the beavers have gnawed through the trunks. Worry has the same effect on us. It will gradually eat away at us until it destroys us.

In addition to telling us not to fret, Psalm 37 gives us positive substitutes for worry. First, it says, "Trust (lean on, rely on, and be confident) in the Lord" (v. 3, AMP). Trust is a matter of not attempting to live an independent life or to cope with difficulties alone. It means going to a greater source for strength.

Second, verse four says, "Delight yourself also in the Lord" (AMP). To delight means to rejoice in God and what He has done for us. Let God supply the joy for your life.

Third, verse five says, "Commit your way to the Lord" (AMP). Commitment is a definite act of the will, and it involves releasing your worries and anxieties to the Lord.

And fourth, we are to "rest in the Lord; wait for Him" (v. 7, AMP). This means to submit in silence to what He ordains but to be ready and expectant for what He is going to do in your life.

Stop worrying and start praying (Philippians 4:6-9; Psalm 34:1-4). The passage in Philippians can be divided into three basic stages. We are given a *premise:* Stop worrying. We are given a *practice:* Start praying. And we are given a *promise:* Peace. The promise is there and available, but we must follow the first two steps in order for the third to occur. We must stop worrying and start praying if we are to begin receiving God's peace.

The results of prayer as a substitute for worry can be vividly seen in a crisis in David's life that prompted him to write Psalm 34. (See 1 Sam. 21:10–22:2.) David had escaped death at the hands of the Philistines by pretending to be insane. He then fled to the cave of Adullam along with four hundred men who were described as distressed, discontented, and in debt. In the midst of all this, David wrote a psalm of praise that begins, "I will bless the Lord at all times; his praise shall continually be in my mouth" (Ps. 34:1, RSV). He did not say he would praise the Lord *sometimes*, but at *all times*, even when his enemies were after him.

How could David bless the Lord in the midst of his life-threatening experience? Because he stopped worrying and started praying: "I sought the Lord, and he answered me, and delivered me from all my fears" (v. 4, RSV). And David didn't turn around and take his cares back after he had deposited them with the Lord. He gave them up. Too many people give their burdens to God with a rubber band attached. As soon as they stop praying, the problems bounce back. They pray, "Give us this day our daily bread," and as soon as they are through praying, they begin to worry where their next meal is going to come from.

Another factor to notice is that God did not take David away from his problem to deliver him from his fears. David was still hiding in the cave with four hundred disgruntled men when he wrote the psalm. God does not always take us out of problematic situations, but he gives us the peace we seek as we proceed prayerfully through each experience. It happened to David, and it happens today to those who pray, unload their cares on God, and leave them there.

Breaking the worry pattern

Again and again the Scriptures give us the answer for fears and worries that stalk us. You may be aware of the resources of Scripture on the subject, but do you know *how* to break the worry pattern in your own life? I'm talking about practical strategies by which you can apply the guidelines of Scripture to your specific worries. Let me share with you a few tips that others have used successfully over the years.

Make a value judgment on worry. Let me illustrate the first suggestion by taking you into my counseling office. I was working with a man who had a roaring tendency to worry. We had talked through the reasons for his worry, and he had tried some of my suggestions for conquering his problem. But it just seemed to me that he was resistant to giving up his worry. This isn't unusual; many people have worried for so long that they have grown comfortable with their negative patterns of thinking. It's actually all they know. They're successful with it and unsure they will be successful with the new style of thinking.

So one day I gave him an assignment that really caught him off guard: "It appears worry is an integral part of your life and that you are determined to keep that tendency. But you only worry periodically throughout the day with no real plan for worrying. So let's set up a definite worry time for you each day instead of spreading it out.

"Tomorrow when you begin to worry about something, instead of worrying at that moment, write down what you're worried about on an index card and keep the card in your pocket. Each time a worry pops up, write it on the card, but don't worry about it yet. Then about 4:00 P.M., go into a room where you can be alone. Sit down, take out the card, and worry about those items as intensely as you can for thirty minutes. Start the next day with a new blank card and do the same thing. What do you think about that idea?"

He stared at me in silence for several moments. "That's got to be one of the dumbest suggestions I've ever heard," he answered finally. "I can't believe I'm paying to hear advice like that."

I smiled and said, "Is it really much different from what you're already doing? Your behavior tells me you like to worry. So I'm just suggesting you put it into a different time frame." As he thought about my comment, he realized I was right: He really *wanted* to worry. And until he decided he didn't want to worry, there was nothing I could do to help him.

This is very important. Unless we make a value judgment on our negative behavior, we will never change. The issue parallels the question Jesus asked the lame man at the pool of Bethesda: "Do you want to become well? [Are you really in earnest about getting well?]" (John 5:6, AMP). We must make some conscious, honest decisions about our worry: Do we like it or dislike it? Is it to our advantage or disadvantage? Is our life better with it or without it? If you're not sure, apply the techniques in this chapter and commit yourself not to worry for a period of just two weeks. Then, from your own experience, decide whether you prefer a life of worry or a life of freedom from worry.

Try a painful reminder. I've run into some very intense worriers whose thought patterns bordered on the obsessive. In a few cases, I've suggested something quite radical for eliminating their negative thoughts.

One such worrier was a young man in his mid-twenties who had literally worried himself into an ulcer. I suggested he place a large, loose rubber band around his wrist. When he started to worry, he was to stretch the rubber band away from his wrist and let it go, snapping himself painfully. For him, continuing to worry was indeed painful.

The next week, he came in and showed me his tender wrists. He felt he needed something radical and that it was effective. Unfortunately, in his case, it was too late. A couple of months later, half his stomach was removed.

Tell yourself to stop. During one session of a Sunday school class I was teaching on the subject of worry, I asked participants to report on an experiment I had suggested the previous week for kicking the worry out of their lives. One woman said she began the experiment Monday morning, and by Friday, she felt the worry pattern that had plagued her for years was finally broken.

What accomplished this radical improvement? It was a simple method of applying God's Word to her life in a new way. I have shared this method with hundreds of people in my counseling office and with thousands in classes and seminars.

Take a blank index card and on one side write the word *STOP* in large, bold letters. On the other side write the complete text of

Philippians 4:6-9. (I especially like the Amplified Version.) Keep the card with you at all times. Whenever you are alone and begin to worry, take the card out, hold the *STOP* side in front of you, and say "Stop!" aloud twice with emphasis. Then turn the card over and read the Scripture passage aloud twice with emphasis.

Taking the card out interrupts your thought pattern of worry. Saying the word "Stop!" further breaks your automatic habit pattern of worry. Then reading the Word of God aloud becomes the positive substitute for worry. If you are in a group of people and begin to worry, follow the same procedure, only do it silently.

The woman who shared in the class said that on the first day of her experiment, she took out the card twenty times during the day. But on Friday she took it out only three times. Her words were, "For the first time in my life, I have the hope that my worrisome thinking can be chased out of my life."

Inventory your worries. Whenever worry plagues you, use some or all of the following suggestions to help you inventory your worries and plan your strategy:

1. Be sure to have your doctor give you a complete physical examination. Have him or her check your glands, vitamin deficiencies, allergies, exercise schedule, and fatigue.

2. Face your worries and admit them when they occur. Don't run from them, for they will return to haunt you. Do not worry about worrying. That just reinforces and perpetuates the problem.

3. Itemize your worries and anxieties on a sheet of paper. Be specific and complete as you describe them.

4. Write down the reasons or causes for your worry. Investigate the sources. Is there any possibility you can eliminate the source or the cause of your worry? Have you tried? What have you tried specifically?

5. Write down the amount of time you spend each day worrying.

6. What has worrying accomplished in your life? Describe the benefits of worrying in detail.

7. Make a list of the following: (a) the ways your worrying has prevented a feared situation from occurring; (b) the ways your worrying increased the problem.

8. If you are nervous or jumpy, try to eliminate any sources of irritation. Stay away from them until you learn how to react differently. For example, if troubling world events worry you, don't watch so many newscasts. Use that time to relax by reading, working in the garden, or riding a bike for several miles. Avoid rushing yourself. If you worry about being late, plan to arrive at a destination early. Give yourself more time.

9. Avoid any type of fatigue—physical, emotional, or intellectual. When you are fatigued, worrisome difficulties can loom out of proportion.

10. When you do get involved in worry, is it over something that really pertains to you and your life, or does it properly belong to someone else? Remember that our fears or worries often may be disguised fears of what others think of us.

11. When a problem arises, face it and decide what you can do about it. Make a list of all of the possible solutions and decide which you think is the best one. If these are minor decisions, make them fairly quickly. Take more time for major decisions.

A worrier usually says, "I go over and over these problems and cannot decide which is best." Look at the facts, then make yourself decide. After you have made your decision, do not question or worry about your choice. Otherwise the worrying pattern erupts all over again. Practice this new pattern of making decisions.

Freedom from worry is possible! It requires that you practice the diligent application of God's Word in your life. This means repetitive behavior. If you fail, don't give up. You may have practiced worrying for many years, and you need to consistently practice the application of Scripture over a long period in order to completely establish a new, worry-free pattern.

TEN

Practical Steps for Overcoming Fear

Our imagination can be a breeding ground for
fear or a channel of God's vision.

Give your fears to God and thank Him in advance
for the peace you are going to experience.

*"Thou dost keep him in perfect peace, whose mind
is stayed on thee."* (Isa. 26:3, RSV)

Have you ever wondered why some people are able to overcome their fears while other people are overcome by their fears?

Terry and Hans, two men I counseled separately, illustrate this contrast. They were from nearly identical backgrounds, and they were both afraid of social activities and interaction.

But that's where their similarities ended. Terry gave in to his fear and, even though he desperately wanted friends and an active social life, he rarely mustered the courage to become involved. Hans, however, faced his fear and refused to be controlled by his emotional thinking. As Hans stood up to his fears, they shrank!

Hans overcame his fears by changing his thought patterns. "When I used to think about getting together with new people," Hans said, "I made all these put-downs about myself, like, 'I'll make a jerk out of myself' or 'No one will like me.' Now when those thoughts pop into my mind and start pumping up my fear, I counter them with realistic, positive thoughts. I think something like, 'I can be friendly and outgoing. People do feel comfortable with me. I can do it.'

"Another thing I often do," Hans continued, "is switch off my negative thoughts, tell myself to relax, take a deep breath, and tense up some muscles and then loosen them. I've found this really helps, because my initial fear response tends to tense me up, even though I may not be fully aware of it. So I make myself become aware of the process and then consciously reverse it. I also spend time rehearsing in my mind how I see myself behaving and responding in a new social setting. I practice my social skills *in advance*, which helps build my confidence." Hans's simple method has worked for many.

Give yourself time to overcome fear

If you have lived with one or more particular fears for a long time, please remember it will take time to overcome it. In fact, even after you have overcome a fear, you may still think you haven't. Does this sound strange? Perhaps, but when you have lived with a fear for so long, it is a major adjustment to begin living without that part of your life. Furthermore, a person who lives with a fear often learns to rely on other people in some way. So giving up that fear also means learning to be more independent.

Most fears need to be overcome gradually. Large or long-established fears are often too overwhelming to be conquered with one swift blow. Trying to conquer the fear immediately may actually cause the fear to grow instead of shrink. The best way to begin overcoming a fear is to face it a little at a time and from a safe distance.

Let's say, for example, that you have a fear of water. Throwing yourself headfirst into a swimming pool might help you overcome your fear. But for most people, the experience would be too traumatic. Wading into the water a little bit deeper each day will probably be more effective in the long run.

Sometimes I hunt pheasants with a large, black Labrador retriever—the kind of dog that often gets excited and jumps on people. Many little children (and some adults) are frightened by these large dogs. The steps for helping a child overcome his fear of a big dog illustrate the gradual approach each of us can use to overcome other fears.

Imagine a four-year-old boy meeting my black Lab for the first time. The huge dog runs up to the boy with his tail wagging and his tongue hanging out of a very large mouth between giant teeth. The dog is just being friendly, but the little boy is terrified by the sight of a dog that appears ready to devour him! The little boy flies to this mother, hides behind her, and cries. The next few times the dog approaches him, the boy has the same fearful reaction.

Then one day, the boy retreats to his mother at the sight of the dog but doesn't cry. The next day, the dog is in the room, and the boy approaches the dog slowly and cautiously with his mother. The child eyes the dog and his big mouth warily from a distance. The boy's mother explains that the dog's mouth is open and his tongue is out because he is smiling and happy. Each day the pair moves two or three steps closer to the dog.

After several days, the boy gingerly puts his hand out and pats the dog's head. The dog's tail wags, and he stretches his neck out so the boy can scratch his head. In time, the boy examines the dog's mouth and teeth and realizes the big, black dog is not going to eat him.

How did the boy overcome his fear? By looking it straight in the mouth and gradually overcoming it! That's not always easy to do, but it brings results.

Sometimes a direct confrontation with fear *will* work to overcome it. I remember a personal story of fear told by Malcolm Boyd, author of *Are You Running with Me, Jesus?* When he was five years old, Malcolm's parents left him with a neighbor for the day. Malcolm did something to upset the neighbor, and her reaction was quite extreme. She struck him on the side of the head and locked him in a dark closet "where a huge white rat will eat you." Young Boyd sat screaming in the darkness waiting for the rat to attack him. And his sense of helplessness and terror at being in the dark persisted into adulthood.

As a middle-aged man, Boyd wanted to rid himself of this troublesome fear. He was asked by some friends to stay in their large and isolated home while they were away. After he moved in, Boyd decided this was the time to face his fear. As darkness fell one evening, he deliberately kept the lights turned off.

When it was totally dark, he could hardly breathe from fear. But he began to feel his way slowly through the rooms of the house. He inched his way from the musty basement to the eerie attic. Gradually, Boyd became accustomed to and comfortable with the dark. His fears diminished, and today they are gone.[1]

As you begin to conquer your fears, be realistic about your expectations. If you were to chart your improvement on a graph, don't expect it would be a straight, upward line of uninterrupted success. Your growth and improvement will come in a series of ups and downs, and there will be times when your fears are actually worse.

You need to anticipate and plan for the down times. If you don't plan for your times of failure, you will be thrown by the apparent reversal in your progress. You will be tempted to think you haven't made any improvement at all, which isn't true. What you choose to focus on in those down moments will affect your whole attitude for the next two days.

If you are coming to grips with a long-standing fear that you have not confronted for many years, things could get worse at first. The fear can actually increase because you are coming closer to it. But overcoming your fear requires that you face and resist the sense of failure you will encounter in the process of getting involved with your fear.

Why don't people try the gradual approach to facing their fears? Because the idea just doesn't occur to them. They are too busy trying to avoid the object or situation that frightens them. And when they do decide to tackle the problem, they think they can lick it immediately, once and for all. The gradual approach to overcoming fear is foreign to many people.

Identify your present fears

If you want to succeed in overcoming your fear, you must develop a strategy for doing so. The first step of this strategy is to specifically identify what you fear.

You may respond, "That's easy; I'm afraid of people." But I'm not sure you are telling me exactly what you are afraid of. Are you afraid of being rejected by people or attacked by people? Are you afraid of what people may think of you? What is it about people that makes you afraid?

Or you say, "I'm afraid to fly." But you still haven't told me exactly what your fear is. Are you afraid of being locked in an airplane's cabin or of being 30,000 feet off the ground or of crashing?

In each generally fearful situation, there can be a number of specific aspects to your fear, and these aspects must be identified. Once you have made specific identification, you can plan a specific strategy. This is part of the process Lloyd Ogilvie suggests when he says: "I confess my fearful imagination and today I ask the Lord to make my imagination a channel of His vision and not a breeding place of fear."[2]

Take a sheet of paper and write down a fear you have. For example, you may state your fear of elevators. Then list all of the different characteristics unique to your fear. You may write that you are afraid of being alone, being up high, falling, being locked in close quarters, meeting a stranger, or being alone with a person of the opposite sex. Some of your fears may have only one or two points, while others may have five or six.

Once you have listed your specific fears, rank them in order of importance, beginning with whatever you fear most.

Describe your fear history

Once you have identified and ranked your fears on a sheet of paper, write down the heading, "Past Experiences with This Fear." Then describe two or three times when you actually experienced this fear. Use the most recent experiences you can remember and give as many details as possible for these encounters. Then compare your description with the list of characteristics you previously identified for this fear to see if they coincide.

Can you remember what you actually said to yourself at the time you experienced your fear? Your statements may have included, "I feel awful," "I wish I was out of here," "This is a terrible experience," or "I can't handle this." Your self-talk under such conditions is very important because you could have inadvertently reinforced your fear response.

Be as specific as possible when listing your reactions to these past fearful situations. Did you become immobilized or did you run? Did you try to remain calm and confront your fear, or did you scream and run away? What did you feel when you last confronted your fear? Did your heart beat faster? Did you perspire? Did you feel like fainting or did your stomach begin to grind? List all the physical symptoms you experienced the last time you met your fear face to face.

On the facing page is a sample chart you can use for the process just described.

Build a fear hierarchy

Regardless of what you fear, you need a plan to help you begin to overcome it. You have identified your fear in specific terms. Your next task is to plan a strategy for gradually approaching it and ultimately mastering it.

The strategy I recommend in this chapter is called building a fear hierarchy. It requires you to use your imagination in approaching the object, situation, or person you fear. You begin by imagining the least threatening situation in which you could involve yourself with this fear object. Gradually you move to the most threatening scenario. Each imaginary scene in between builds upon those previous to it.

Here are two sample fear hierarchies that illustrate a gradual, scene-by-scene approach to overcoming fear. Notice how each hierarchy begins with a low-threat scene and moves toward a direct confrontation with fear.

Fear Hierarchy for Overcoming the Fear of Flying in Airplanes

1. I look at an advertisement for an airplane flight to Europe.
2. I look at color pictures of airplanes.
3. I visit an airport and look at the planes. While I am there, I see a friend or relative board a plane to go on vacation.
4. I call an airline to practice getting flight information.

1. The object of my fear is . . .

2. The important characteristics of what I fear are (ranked in order of importance) . . .
   a.
   b.
   c.
   d.
   e.
   f.
   g.
   h.

3. My past experience with this fear is . . .

4. My reactions to my fear were . . .
   a. What I said . . .

   b. What I did . . .

   c. What I felt . . .

5. How fearful was I? (Circle the number that best represents how you feel in
the fearful situation: 1 means little or no fear; 5 means moderate fear; 10
means extreme fear.)

1	2	3	4	5	6	7	8	9	10

5. I arrange with a local pilot to visit the airport and see a
small private plane.

6. I visit the airport and see the planes. I sit inside the pilot's
small plane while the engine is running. There is no attempt
to fly the plane. I just get comfortable sitting in the cabin.

7. I imagine myself on a commercial jet plane getting ready for takeoff. The details for this and the remaining scenes I imagine are provided by a friend or relative who enjoys flying.
8. I imagine myself on a jet while it is in flight. I am with several friends or relatives.
9. I imagine myself on a jet while it is in flight. I am by myself.
10. I imagine myself on a jet while it is in flight. I am by myself, and the ride is somewhat bumpy.
11. I imagine myself on a jet by myself, and the plane is landing.
12. I take a short plane flight with a friend or relative.

Fear Hierarchy for Overcoming the Fear of the Dark

1. I am in a room with a friend and the lighting is fairly dim.
2. My friend and I light two candles, and I turn off all the electric lights.
3. My friend and I are in the room together, and I blow out one of candles.
4. My friend and I are in the room together. My friend blows out the remaining candle, and we talk to each other while the room is dark. After five seconds my friend turns on an electric light.
5. My friend and I repeat scene 4, but this time we don't talk.
6. My friend and I repeat scene 5, but this time we wait a full minute before turning on the light.
7. My friend and I repeat scene 6, but this time we wait five minutes before turning on the light.
8. I am alone in the room, and the electric lighting is dim.
9. I am alone in the room, and there are only two candles lit.
10. I am alone in the room, and there is only one candle lit.
11. I am alone in the room, and there is only one candle lit. I call my friend on the phone, blow out the candle, and talk for a couple of minutes. Then I turn on the electric light and finish my phone conversation.

12. I am alone in the room, and there is one candle lit. I blow it out and wait five seconds before I turn on the electric light.
13. I repeat step 12, but this time I wait twenty seconds.
14. I repeat step 12, but this time I wait a full minute.
15. I repeat step 12, but this time I wait five full minutes.[3]

Remember that the fear hierarchy is a mental exercise; you are not facing the actual fear. And notice from the samples that the number of scenes may vary depending on how many you need to construct for your own mental exercise. The more gradual the approach to the fear, the more scenes you will want to include in your imagination.

It is vital to add one additional procedure to each step in your fear hierarchy. Recommit your fear to our Lord at each level, and thank Him for giving you the peace you are going to experience. Ask Him to make your imagination a residence for His peace and presence.

In creating scenes for a fear hierarchy, some people choose to visualize an imaginary venture instead of a real-life sequence of events. For some, to rehearse the "real thing" is too much of a threat at first, so they choose to imagine a safer scene. This is a perfectly acceptable step in overcoming fears gradually.

The types of scenes you include in your hierarchy will depend on your own circumstances and fears. For example, you can include in your imaginary scenes friends, relatives, or whoever you need to provide support and help in overcoming your fear. As you create a scene in your mind, begin with one that is only slightly unsettling to you. The fear must be small enough for you to be able to eliminate it in your mind and stay relaxed during this process. If your first scene creates too much fear and anxiety for you, back off and create one that is less stressful.

Here is an additional example. John was a college student who was petrified to speak in front of a class or a group at church. He wanted to be a schoolteacher, so he knew something had to be done to eliminate his fear. He committed himself to a program of creating visual imagery. Notice how John gradually builds up to a very fear-provoking situation for his final scene. Here is his list:

Fear Hierarchy for Overcoming the Fear of Speaking to Groups

1. I imagine myself reading from a book out loud with no one else in the room or likely to walk into the room while I am reading.
2. I imagine myself giving a practice lecture out loud at home when no one else is present and no one is likely to walk in.
3. I see myself recording my voice as I talk out loud. Then I listen to myself in the safety of my room and list every positive point that I can about my presentation.
4. I see myself reading to my best friend out loud, and he keeps giving me compliments.
5. I practice reading out loud to three friends in my room for fifteen minutes.
6. I practice giving a brief lecture on the meaning of a passage of Scripture to one of my close friends in my room. Afterwards, he helps me with some suggestions, then I repeat the presentation, adding his suggestions.
7. I imagine myself giving this same presentation to several of my friends in my room. I see myself starting out a bit uptight, but then I relax and pretty soon there is no tension. The presentation goes quite well. Each friend tells me that I did a good job, and I feel good about the presentation.
8. I imagine myself filling in for one of the teachers at church in a high school class of five students. I see myself being not too nervous. After I meet each student, I give a brief devotional, and they listen to me. It goes quite well.
9. I attend a college conference with my friends. During an open meeting, I raise my hand and share my thoughts, which I have just rehearsed in my mind. Other people are interested and attentive to me, and then my friends all give me their responses.
10. I continue to speak up at meetings and set a goal of speaking at least three times in each meeting.

Your fear-reducing scenario

Now it is time for you to begin this exercise. Copy the following fear hierarchy outline on a separate sheet of paper, leaving plenty of space to write for each scene. List one personal fear you would like to eliminate from your life. Then briefly sketch in as many verbal scenes as you need to move you gradually from a safe scene to a solid confrontation with your fear. Don't be concerned if you have difficulty relaxing during the final scenes. This will come later as you mentally rehearse the whole process.

Fear Hierarchy for Overcoming the Fear of _____
(your fear).

Scene 1 (Remember: This scene should be very safe and simple with very little anxiety):

Scene 2:

Scene 3:

Scene 4:

Scene 5:

Scene 6:

Scene 7:

Scene 8:

Scene 9:

Scene 10:

(Continue with as many scenes as you need.)

The Final Scene (This scene should be one that could make you anxious or fearful if you actually performed it at this time.):

Now, go back through what you have written and add specific details to make the imaginary experience even more realistic. For example, imagine you have just arrived at Niagara Falls. Close your eyes and picture yourself at one of the viewing points. Imagine the scene as vividly as you can. Hold this image for fifteen seconds. What was it like? Did you hear the roar of the water cascading down? Did you feel the breeze blowing and the mist on the air? What did the sky look like? Were there clouds, or was the sky clear? Were there other people around, or were you alone? How did you feel as you viewed this spectacular sight? Now perhaps you have an idea of what I mean by adding more details to your step-by-step scenario.

If the scenes you created are not based on a real event, it is important you see yourself as an active participant. And if they are real-life scenes, you must be an active participant in them as well. Be sure you don't just sit on the outside and observe as these scenes are passing through your mind. Put yourself into the scene as though you were actually there.

Here is an example of greater detail in John's revised plan for overcoming his fear of speaking in front of groups:

Fear Hierarchy for Overcoming the Fear of Speaking to Groups (Revised)

1. I am alone in my room at the dorm. Standing in the middle of the room, I read out loud from three pages of a devotional book that I enjoy. I stand up straight, use proper breathing, and change my volume and tone of voice.

2. Now I use this same book as a resource, but this time I give a spontaneous talk as though I were speaking to other students or a class. I imagine that people are in my room, and I look from chair to chair as though each chair were filled. I try to feel what it would be like if there were real bodies there.

3. I now read or repeat to myself several passages of Scripture that remind me of the presence of God and the power of Jesus Christ in my life. I repeat Philippians 4:13, "I can do everything through him who gives me strength" and Jeremiah 33:3, "Call to me and I will answer you and tell you great and unsearchable things you do not know." I visualize Jesus Christ standing with me as I speak, and I continue to remind myself of His presence with me.

4. I repeat step 2, but this time I record my presentation and my friend listens to it. I make a list of what I can do to improve it and give the devotional talk once again.

5. Now I am going to read out loud again. But this time my friend is there, and he is sitting about six feet in front of me. He is very relaxed, and an encouraging smile is on his face.

6. This time I am going to read again, but there are three of my friends sprawled about in my room. I am still somewhat comfortable. I relax, and before I begin I repeat the verses from step 3 concerning the presence and power of Christ.

7. Now I am back with my one friend, and this time I am giving a talk without notes. I talk for several minutes in a casual way, sharing what I remember from the book. Afterward, he gives me his positive suggestions, and I repeat the presentation.

8. I am at church, and I walk into a classroom where I am substituting for another teacher. I introduce myself to the students, and we chat for a bit. I see myself asking a very pertinent question to get their attention. I share my devotional with them. Not only are they interested, but they ask some insightful questions.

9. I repeat step 3.

10. I attend the college briefing conference at Forest Home

Conference Center. I am in a group meeting of fifty students, and a discussion is in progress. I raise my hand to be recognized, then stand and share my thoughts on the topic at hand. People watch and listen, some nod in agreement, and there is general interest in what I say to them.

Positive self-talk

You have taken a tremendous step forward by creating your own fear hierarchy and filling it with details. This exercise will help you approach your fear in a very gradual manner. But there is one more step you must take that has to do with your self-talk or inner conversations. What you say to yourself at this time may make the difference between overcoming your fear and continuing to be overcome by it.

If your statements reflect negativism, you will not mature in your mastery over fear. For example, if John says, "I'm going to forget what I wanted to say and make a jerk of myself," or "I will never learn to talk in front of people," or "This is going to be too much for me," he will hinder his progress. But if he counters each negative statement with a positive alternative, he will relax. John could say, "This is a new situation, and I will learn how to handle it," or "I probably won't forget what I am going to say, and even if I do, I can just say I have frequent lapses of memory like most geniuses," or "I've learned all of my life, and it may take awhile, but I'll get there."

I have one more list for you—your self-talk list. On the left side, list some of the typical negative statements you make whenever you find yourself in the situation you fear. Then on the right side list the statements you could make that will help you cope with the situation and face your fear. (For an example of negative and positive self-talk, see page 91 in chapter 6.)

True, this exercise is a bit complex and involves a lot of effort. But for many this process has been very effective. It is a step toward overcoming your fear. And your fears *can* be overcome; that's a promise from God!

Self-talk

Past Negative Statements	Present and Future Positive Statements
1.	1.
2.	2.
3.	3.
4.	4.
5.	5.
6.	6.
7.	7.
8.	8.

Final Thoughts

———

There are times in your life when you experience fears that motivate you to work creatively. And there are times in your life when you experience fears that cripple your productivity and switch your life to slow motion.

Have you ever considered the question, "Why did God put so many 'fear nots' in the Bible when He knows we tend to be fearful creatures?" God's "fear nots" are just another way by which He has provided for you. God doesn't want your life to be a chore. Fear makes it that. God doesn't want you to be driven by fear but by hope. And He gives you the hope you need when He says, "Fear not."

You can be a free person without compromising who you are out of fear of others. Life is a risk, but risks give you a great opportunity to learn to live by faith. Fear will no longer be the dominating force in your life if you refuse to let it be. Your imagination is one of God's greatest gifts to you. Use it! Your imagination can generate fear—or it can be a vehicle for bringing God's peace and calm into your life. Isaiah the prophet said, "Thou dost keep him in perfect peace, whose mind is stayed on thee" (Isa. 26:3, RSV).

Recently I was privileged to meet a pastor's wife, the author of a very inspiring article about a letter she wrote to her children.

148

The letter expressed how she was once again struggling with cancer. In one part of her letter she talked about fear:

> Fear has knocked at my door. Sometimes in the past five days, I have let fear in for awhile. It has not been good. I have thought of silly things like: I can't wear that new spring suit we just bought on sale or that lovely wool skirt we've waited six months for. Other times I think how much I want to see Kathy graduate, go off to Bible school, fall in love with the finest Christian man this world has ever seen, and then watch her walk down the aisle on her dad's arm. Then I think I want to see Kim married and settled. Finally, for sure, I would like grandchildren.
>
> But, dear children of mine, these are human thoughts, and to dwell on them is not healthy. I know one of the strongest desires God has given us is the desire to live, but I want to say to God that I trust Him in this too. My vision is so limited. These human desires are the purest on earth, but—if I had even a tiny glimpse of heaven, I wouldn't want to stay here. Because I am human, I do. So I have decided that I will put a "no trespassing" sign at the entrance of the path of human desires and not let my thoughts wander down it.
>
> When fear knocks, it is my determined choice to let faith answer the door, faith that is settled on the sure promises of the Word of God. [1]

God says, "Fear not." Why? "For I am with you. . . . I have redeemed you; I have called you by name, you are mine" (Isa. 41:10; 43:1).

You are His! You can live your life free from fear!

Notes

Chapter 1

1. John Haggai, *How to Win over Fear* (Eugene, Oreg.: Harvest House, 1987), 73.
2. Herbert Fensterheim and Jean Baer, *Stop Running Scared* (New York: Dell, 1978), adapted from pp. 50-52.
3. Paul Tournier, *The Strong and the Weak* (Philadelphia: Westminster, 1963), 93.
4. Joseph Wolpe and David Wolpe, *Our Useless Fears* (Boston: Houghton Mifflin, 1981), adapted from pp. 1-14.

Chapter 2

1. Dr. Herbert Benson, *The Mind-Body Effect* (New York: Berkley Publishing, 1980).
2. Fensterheim and Baer, adapted from pp. 41-42.
3. Susan Jeffers, *Feel the Fear and Do It Anyway* (New York: Fawcett Book Group, 1987), adapted from pp. 39-43.

Chapter 3

1. David Viscott, *I Love You, Let's Work It Out* (New York: Simon and Schuster, 1987), adapted from pp. 123-127.
2. Lloyd John Ogilvie, *12 Steps to Living without Fear* (Waco, Tex.: Word, 1987), 133.

Chapter 4

1. Dr. Connell Cowan and Dr. Melvyn Kinder, *Women Men Love—Women Men Leave* (New York: New American Library, 1987), adapted from p. 30.
2. Mike Mason, *The Mystery of Marriage* (Portland, Oreg.: Multnomah, 1985), 84.
3. Michael McGill, *The McGill Report on Male Intimacy* (San Francisco: Harper and Row, 1985), adapted from pp. 220-231.
4. McGill, adapted from pp. 245-246.
5. Tim Timmons and Charlie Hedges, *Call It Love or Call It Quits* (Fort Worth, Tex.: Worthy Publishing, 1988), adapted from pp. 122-128.
6. David Viscott, *Risking* (New York: Pocket Books, 1979), adapted from pp. 64-68.
7. Viscott, adapted from pp. 75-79.

Chapter 5

1. Ogilvie, *12 Steps*, 112.
2. Dr. William J. Knaus, *Do It Now* (Englewood Cliffs, N.J.: Prentice-Hall, 1979), adapted from pp. 64-71.
3. J. I. Packer, *Knowing God* (Downers Grove, Ill.: InterVarsity, 1973), 87.
4. Joseph Cooke, *Free for the Taking* (Old Tappan, N.J.: Fleming H. Revell, 1975), 29.
5. David Burns, *Feeling Good* (New York: Signet Books, 1980), 258.
6. Frank Houghton, *Amy Carmichael of Dohnavur* (Fort Washington, Penn.: Christian Literature Crusade, 1979).
7. Ogilvie, *12 Steps*, 109.

Chapter 6

1. Lloyd John Ogilvie, *Why Not Accept Christ's Healing and Wholeness?* (Old Tappan, N.J.: Fleming H. Revell, 1985), 162.
2. H. Norman Wright, *How to Have a Creative Crisis* (Waco, Tex.: Word, 1986), adapted from chapter 1. Also: Stephen Gullo and Connie Church, *Loveshock: How to Survive a Broken Heart and Love Again* (New York: Simon and Schuster, 1988), adapted from pp. 31-48.

3. Gene Emery, *A New Beginning: How You Can Change Your Thoughts through Cognitive Therapy* (New York: Simon and Schuster, 1981), 61.

Chapter 7

1. Herbert Fensterheim and Jean Baer, *Making Life Right When It Feels All Wrong* (New York: Rawson Associates, 1988), adapted from pp. 4-7.
2. For additional information on this subject, see chapter 8 in my book *Understanding the Man in Your Life* (Word Books).
3. Georgia Watkin-Lanoil, *The Female Stress Syndrome* (New York: Berkley, 1985), adapted from p. 73.
4. Dr. David Stoop, *Living with a Perfectionist* (Nashville: Thomas Nelson, 1987), adapted from p. 17.
5. Lloyd John Ogilvie, *Lord of the Impossible* (Nashville: Abingdon, 1984), 90.
6. David Seamands, *Healing Grace* (Wheaton, Ill.: Victor Books, 1988), adapted from pp. 61-66.
7. Seamands, 117.
8. Seamands, 115-116.
9. For additional assistance in your struggle with perfection, see chapter 7 of my book *Making Peace with Your Past* (Revell).
10. Ogilvie, *Lord of the Impossible*, 70.
11. Ogilvie, *Lord of the Impossible*, adapted from pp. 92-95.
12. David Burns, *Feeling Good* (New York: Signet Books, 1980), adapted from pp. 325-326.
13. Susan Jeffers, *Feel the Fear* (New York: Fawcett Book Group, 1987), adapted from pp. 112-126.
14. Stewart Emery, *Actualizations* (Garden City, N.Y.: Dolphin Books, 1978).

Chapter 8

1. Malcolm Boyd, "How I Overcame Three Fears," *Parade*, 3 July 1988, adapted from p. 11.
2. A helpful book to read is my *Making Peace with Your Past* (Revell).
3. Jane Burks and Lenora Yuen, *Procrastination* (Reading, Mass.: Addison-Wesley, 1984), adapted from pp. 29-41.

Chapter 9
1. Original source unknown.
2. John Haggai, *How to Win over Worry* (Eugene, Oreg.: Harvest House, 1987), 16-17.
3. O. Quentin Hyder, *The Christian's Handbook of Psychiatry* (Old Tappan, N.J.: Fleming H. Revell, 1971).
4. Earl Lee, *Recycled for Living* (Ventura, Calif.: Regal Books, 1973), 4.
5. Samuel H. Kraines and Eloise S. Thetford, *Help for the Depressed* (Springfield, Ill.: Charles C. Thomas, 1979), 190-191.

Chapter 10
1. Malcolm Boyd, adapted from p. 11.
2. Lloyd John Ogilvie, *12 Steps*, 147.
3. Gerald Rosen, *Don't Be Afraid* (Englewood Cliffs, N.J.: Prentice-Hall, 1976), 69-71.

Final Thoughts
1. Shirley Unrau, "Learning with a Dying Mother," *Confident Living*, December 1987, 20-22.